About the Author

D ONALD WARD is an editor and journalist who
has worked in western Canada all his life. He has
published nonfiction, poetry, short stories, and essays,
and has edited more than a dozen books dealing with
western Canadian issues. He lives in Saskatoon with his
wife, Colleen, and their two daughters, Brigid and Caitlin.

The People

A Historical Guide to the First Nations
of Alberta, Saskatchewan, and Manitoba

D ONALD W ARD

FIFTH
HOUSE
PUBLISHERS

Front cover painting, *Many Chiefs–Piegan Indian,* by James Henderson
reproduced courtesy Glenbow-Alberta Institute/61.49.2
Back cover photograph, "Cree Indians," by Charles W. Mathers,
reproduced courtesy Provincial Archives of Alberta/B.766
Cover design by Sandra Hastie/GDL

The publisher gratefully acknowledges the support received from The Canada
Council, Heritage Canada, and the Saskatchewan Arts Board. Thanks are also due
to Brock Silversides of the Provincial Archives of Alberta, the Royal Saskatchewan
Museum, the Glenbow-Alberta Institute, the Saskatchewan Archives Board,
the Provincial Archives of Manitoba, the City of Vancouver Archives, and
the National Archives of Canada for their assistance with photo research.

Printed and bound in Canada by Friesens, Altona, MB
06 / 7 6 5 4
CANADIAN CATALOGUING IN PUBLICATION DATA
Ward, Donald B. (Donald Bruce), 1952–

The people : a historical guide to the first nations
of Alberta, Saskatchewan, and Manitoba

Includes bibliographical references.
ISBN 1-895618-56-8
1. Indians of North America - Prairie Provinces - History. I. Title
E78.P7W37   1995   971.2'00497   C94-920275-4

FIFTH HOUSE LTD.

Contents

....

For Colleen, with love

Acknowledgements

....

N O BOOK comes to publication by the efforts of the author alone. As an editor, in fact, I have sometimes wished we could dispense with authors entirely. As an author, however, I am deeply grateful to the people whose effortless professionalism has helped bring *The People* to this point. Dr. Margaret Hanna's exhaustive critique of an early draft of the introduction had the salutary effect of realigning my thoughts on several key issues. The distinguished historian J.R. Miller read the manuscript and offered valuable advice, both historical and literary, which I have taken with gratitude. Finally, Charlene Dobmeier has been a patient, generous, and perceptive editor; I give thanks for her gentle persistence and her expertise.

Approximate Tribal Distributions

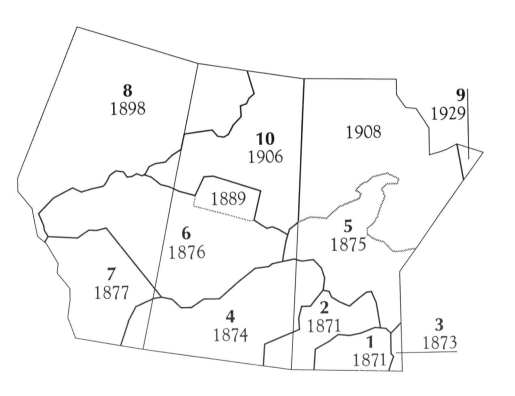

Numbered Treaties

"What is life? It is as the little shadow
that runs across the grass
and loses itself in the sunset."

....

– Crowfoot

Introduction

I N THE BEGINNING Napiwa, the Old Man, created the island from a grain of sand he took from the muskrat's paw. He sent a young wolf to find the edge of the island, but the wolf died of old age before it got there. Then Nanoss, the Old Woman, said to Napiwa, "Your island is vast and beautiful, but something is missing. It needs to be filled with people."

"Let it be so," said Napiwa, "but I shall have the first word."

"And I," said Nanoss, "shall have the last."

Napiwa wanted humankind to be made of wood and grow like trees, but Nanoss said they should be made of flesh and reproduce their kind like animals. Napiwa said they should have square faces with vertical mouths and an ear on each side of the nose, but Nanoss said they should have round faces with horizontal mouths, and their ears should be on the sides of their heads so they could hear their enemies coming without getting their noses full of dirt. Napiwa said that humankind, man and woman, should live forever and never part, but Nanoss said it was better if they died; otherwise the island might become overcrowded and there wouldn't be enough food for everyone. And so Napiwa created death, and Nanoss said, "Now people will have a little sympathy for one another."

In the Peigan creation myth, the "island" is the earth. More specifically, it is that portion of the earth that had been given to them in stewardship: the Great Plains. It was a landscape large enough to hold most of Europe. Spreading west from southern Manitoba to the Rocky Mountains, and from the North Saskatchewan River south into Texas, it was a land so vast and rich in resources that it beggared the imaginations of those who came to trade and to settle. The historian W.L. Morton has called it "the processed outcome of a majestic evolutionary logic." To those who had lived and flourished here for twelve thousand years, it was the island, their sacred earth, and they resented the intrusions of the white man.

To the north were the regions of the subarctic: the boreal forest and the tundra, stretching east from the interior of Alaska to Hudson Bay. It was a land of lakes, rivers, and muskeg, of long, cruel winters and brief, warm summers. "Summer such as it is, comes at once," wrote David Thompson, "and with it myriads of tormenting Mosketoes; the air is thick with them, there is no cessation day or night of suffering from them . . . " Despite the "Mosketoes," the western subarctic has been inhabited longer than any other part of Canada. For it was here that the first ones came when they crossed from Asia.

From the eastern tip of Siberia to the western tip of Alaska is a mere sixty-eight kilometres, and there are two islands halfway across where a migrating band might camp overnight. Inuit from both sides still make the journey in open boats. It isn't hard to imagine an entire civilization paddling over, or walking across a land bridge, if they took a few thousand years to do it. What is hard to imagine is their motivation, for Asia was hardly overcrowded at the time, and the climate would not change dramatically in sixty-eight kilometres.

But their motives were largely irrelevant. They didn't know they were migrating as their territory expanded year by year, generation after generation. The land bridge across the Bering Strait was in fact a continent, Beringia. Over thousands of years, glaciation lowered the seas by ninety metres or more, creating a region much like the modern plains, with open spaces and grazing animals. Many of the animals were related to modern species, although the fossil record indicates that they were much larger: moose three metres high, giant long-horned buffalo, beavers the size of bears, hairy mammoths and mastodons, horses, and camels.

Like their descendants, the people were hunters and gatherers. They gathered plants for eating, flavouring, making tools, and medicinal purposes. They were skilled in the arts of fishing, making fire, weaving baskets, and twisting fibres into rope. They invented the canoe and the snowshoe, and crafted them with great skill. The dog was their only domestic animal. With weapons of wood and stone, they killed the massive creatures that roamed the woodlands or grazed in the open spaces, and hunted smaller game with spears or trapped them with snares. More important than weapons and tools was the knowledge of the animal and the terrain, and especially the spiritual connection of the hunter with the hunted. For in their scheme of things, creation was a unity of the created: all plants,

Prehistoric arrowhead. *Royal Saskatchewan Museum 94–254–02*

animals, and inanimate objects had spirits or souls, and humankind did not hold a privileged place among them.

By the time Beringia was exposed completely, at least two thousand years had passed. To the people who had been gradually incorporating it into their territory, it was as if it had always been there. Just as gradually, the glaciers retreated, and Beringia was swallowed by the sea. By that time people were inhabiting the coasts of North and South America, and a continental trade network was already in place.

No one knows exactly how long people have been living in the Americas. Estimates of thirty thousand to one hundred thousand years have been largely discounted. So, too, have the rather attractive theories of the American archæologist Jeffrey Goodman, who proposed that humankind had evolved in southern California about seventy thousand years ago and then migrated to Asia. Radiocarbon dating has failed to find any evidence of human habitation in North America more than twelve thousand years old. On the other hand, evidence that many archæologists consider equally convincing places humankind in the "New World," specifically in the western subarctic, at least twenty-five thousand years ago.

The term "New World" is, of course, problematic. The distinguished historian Olive Patricia Dickason has written, "The world that Europeans labelled 'New' when they became aware of it in the fifteenth century has turned out to be anything but new," and the peoples who lived here "have a history that can claim the dignified label of 'ancient.'"

In the subarctic, these ancient peoples left the traces of their passing.

Most of their campsites were small, and many have been disturbed or destroyed by frost and weather. Others are shallow, and hidden by forests. Even so, there is a clear record of climatic change and migration, and of regional diversity in tools, technologies, and subsistence strategies. About forty-five hundred years ago, for example, a warmer climate coaxed southern plains-dwellers into the subarctic. A thousand years later, a colder climate influenced the movement of people from the Hudson Bay coast inland to Manitoba and as far west as Lake Athabasca in Saskatchewan. Another millennium later, a warming trend brought people north again.

While most of the archæological sites that have been discovered are small, there are exceptions. One site on Southern Indian Lake on the Churchill River in northern Manitoba takes in some eight hectares; others are deeply stratified, indicating several thousand years of occupation. Archæological complexes across the Northwest Territories and northern Alberta, Saskatchewan, and Manitoba indicate the arrival of the ancestors of the Dene some twenty-six hundred years ago. The Selkirk Composite, an archæological complex dating from a thousand years ago, is taken to represent the ancestors of the present-day Cree.

On the plains, too, history is written in the campsites and the ceremonial places. Paleo-Indians, identified by their distinctive spear points, inhabited the area between 9500 and 5500 B.C. During this time the landscape changed from spruce forests and glacial lakes to grasslands and rolling hills, and the enormous mammals either suffered extinction or were supplanted by their modern forms. Some time between 5500 B.C. and A.D. 100 the developing human culture produced the *atlatl,* or spear thrower, along with a light throwing dart that was not quite an arrow. During a long, hot, dry season known as the altithermal period (5000 B.C. –2500 B.C.), the grasslands expanded to the north and east, and life became more difficult for humans and animals alike. For some twenty-five hundred years, the northern plains were severely depopulated. People seem to have moved, for the most part, into the foothills or the river valleys, or into the parklands to the north and east of the plains. Even so, a variety of archæological sites from this period, including rock shelters, buffalo kill sites and processing areas, burial sites, and quarries, clearly show that the plains were never abandoned.

After a few millennia the climate evolved to its present state and the grasslands assumed their present boundaries. Some time after A.D. 100 the plains cultures developed the bow and arrow. While not necessarily more efficient than the atlatl and dart, the knowledge necessary to acquire the new technology is indicative of the growing sophistication of the culture. So, too, is the development of pottery, which revolutionized cooking for a time. Many cultures later switched back to vessels of hide because it was difficult to transport pottery by horse travois. But for a time, at least, meat and vegetables could be cooked without using hot rocks, and the absence of grit in the daily menu no doubt made all food more palatable. Horticulture was also practised, and while earthlodge villages were not common on the plains, they were not unknown. The explorer and mapmaker Peter Fidler reported finding the remains of one village along the South Saskatchewan River.

An extensive trade network had been in place since earliest times. Flint from North Dakota was regularly traded into Saskatchewan and Manitoba, as was pipestone from Minnesota and Wisconsin. Copper tools from the

Old Woman's Phase pottery, about seven hundred years old. *Royal Saskatchewan Museum 94-254-16*

Lake Superior region made their way to Manitoba, Saskatchewan, and Alberta some five thousand years ago. Shells from the Gulf of Mexico and the coast were to be found on the plains twenty-five hundred years ago. And within fifty years of Columbus's landing, European trade goods turned up in what is now Saskatchewan.

Sacred places show up in the archæological record almost as frequently as campsites, both on the plains and in the subarctic. First Nations cultures revolve around the sacred, around the kinship of all things, animate and inanimate, with one another and with that uncreated spirit the Judæo-Christian tradition names God. Several dozen medicine wheels, structures as old and mysterious as Stonehenge, have been found on hilltops above the prairie in Alberta and Saskatchewan. Pictographs, some of them quite recent, are to be found all along the Churchill River; the canoeist approaching Medicine Rapids is struck by the simple beauty of what appears to be a natural altar, and the painted figure—probably less than two hundred years old—that seems to float on the rock face above it. Petroforms and petroglyphs are also common throughout the western interior, and sometimes whole geographical areas, such as the Great Sand Hills and the Missouri Coteau, were and are held sacred.

To these cultures, in the mid-eighteenth century, came the horse. Within a generation, many of the plains nations were superb riders. They acquired firearms at about the same time, and the stage was set for what some early historians characterized as the "perfection" of high plains culture. It is worth remembering, however, that archæologists, anthropologists, and historians did not attempt to fully describe the First Nations of Canada until the twentieth century, and much remains still to be learned. By the time historians and social scientists came on the scene, in fact, the original peoples had all changed dramatically from the life of even a hundred years before. What many history books define as "traditional" plains culture, then, was in fact a blending of cultures, and comparatively new to all of them. What remained unchanged, and endures to this day, was the spiritual core, the social structures, the importance of the family and the elders in day-to-day existence.

The life of the First Nations of the plains and the subarctic revolved around the hunt, not the hunter—a point overlooked by many European observers. Women were not simply the servants of the warrior class, cheap manual labour to process dead animals. They were providers in their own right, and they have their honoured place in ceremony and story. It is women who bring forth life. This power alone was sufficient to inspire awe among the wise. But women were involved at every level of community life and on every plane of existence. The complementarity of man and woman is acknowledged in virtually every ceremony of every nation. In many cases, the wisdom of the elders was the wisdom of the women. Who can tell how often that wisdom prevailed, how many times a hunt was successful, how often a band was diverted from a disastrous course of action because of the overarching prudence and concern of women? It was something the men took for granted, perhaps, and historians, for the most part, did not record.

It is difficult in a work of this length not to make sweeping generalizations or to seem to emphasize one aspect of First Nations culture over another. The work is brief, and focusses primarily on the past three hundred years. During this period, all peoples had many elements in common, but there were as many, often subtler, points of difference.

To speak of the horse coming to the Blackfoot is, in a sense, to speak of the horse coming to the Cree, the Assiniboine, the Sarcee, the Saulteaux, or the Shoshoni, but the horse was more common among some nations than others, and it was valued in different ways. To describe the Cree hunting buffalo is to describe the Peigan and the Blood, the Dakota, or the Crow, but again, the manner in which this all-important animal was integrated spiritually and conceptually with the life of the people varied widely. Similarly, to examine the spirituality of the Slavey is to gain insight into the belief systems of the Chipewyan, the Beaver, and the Sekani,

Quartz buffalo effigy, between four hundred and a thousand years old. *Royal Saskatchewan Museum 94-0473-01*

without necessarily learning anything about the unique expressions of each group. And if you begin to question who was affected by the fur trade, the answer must involve every sentient human being within the boundaries of Manitoba, Saskatchewan, Alberta and beyond, and a billion fur-bearing animals besides.

The story of the First Nations of the interior from the time of European contact to the end of the nineteenth century, and sometimes beyond, runs parallel with the story of the fur trade. The Natives had been trading among themselves for millennia, but it was the arrival of Europeans with their valuable trade goods that more or less dictated the commercial course of the North American continent for two hundred years. "The fur trade," wrote Sylvia Van Kirk in *Many Tender Ties*, "forms the basis of recorded history in Western Canada." It fuelled the explorations of the French and the English alike, and gave rise to several commercial empires, at least one of which was directed by powerful Native interests.

But the fur trade was not merely an economic activity dictated by the sartorial tastes of western Europe; it was a social and cultural phenomenon as well. "The growth of a mutual dependency between Indian and European trader at the economic level," Van Kirk pointed out, "could not help but engender a significant cultural exchange as well." The result was a "unique society" based on "both Indian and European customs and technology." Intermarriage between traders and Native women was common, and incorporated customs from both cultures. A Native woman thus married played a pivotal role between two cultures, advancing the interests of her people among the traders, and advancing the traders' interests among her people. What emerged was a distinct society, neither European nor entirely Native, in which family life was treasured.

It is worth remembering, however, that the early accounts of traders and explorers, whether they were married to Native women or not, are not free of bias and distortion, errors of fact, misunderstandings, or misinterpretations. The historical record is overflowing with the journals and letters of Europeans who were determined to record in detail everything they saw. But they weren't always reliable. Some arrived with their expectations and prejudices fully formed, and saw more or less what they wanted to see: savagery, naïveté, greed, promiscuity. A man who was expecting vulgar displays of sexuality would have no trouble believing that every attractive woman he met was trying to lure him into an illicit relationship. Similarly, people who witnessed young Blackfoot warriors piercing their chests with skewers did not hesitate to character-

Stone "plate" with incised turtle, four hundred to a thousand years old. *Royal Saskatchewan Museum 94-0473-03*

ize it as "self torture" and the Sun Dance as a "savage" ceremony, never thinking that the Blackfoot might well have described the circumcision of an infant in the same terms.

Perhaps Chipewyan women, then, did not suffer a life of such drudgery as Samuel Hearne and David Thompson reported. Perhaps infanticide and blood-feuds were the practices of a few bands and not a whole society. Perhaps what was ancient and enduring in the plains cultures was not the brief glory of the mounted warrior with a Winchester repeater, but their faith, their language, and their art—and the buffalo, the sacred beast that defined them more surely than horses and guns ever could. Whether they spoke Algonquian, Athapaskan, Siouan, or Kootenaian, the First Nations of Canada had no written language that the white man could understand. Their history was being recorded in a way that made sense to them—in pictographs and petroglyphs, in oral accounts passed from one generation to another—but the history books have been written by others. We cannot assume that we have not missed a nuance or a shade of meaning that would turn our understanding upside down.

At the time of the French exploration, virtually every part of what was to become Canada was claimed or occupied by one or another aboriginal nation. With fifty-three distinct indigenous languages, not including French and English, Canada was and is one of the most complex linguistic and cultural regions on earth. Six languages are represented in the history and the diverse territories enclosed by the borders of Alberta, Saskatchewan, and Manitoba. The Blackfoot, the Cree, the Saulteaux, and the Gros Ventre speak Algonquian. The Assiniboine, the Dakota, and the Crow speak Siouan. Kootenaian is a language isolate, spoken only by the Kootenay. The Iroquois who came to work for the North West Company in the late eighteenth century speak Iroquoian, and the Shoshoni, long departed from the Canadian plains, speak an Uto-Aztecan language.

To the north are the nations of the subarctic: the Woodland Cree, the Chipewyan, the Beaver, the Slavey, and the Sekani. With the exception of the Cree, these peoples are all Athapaskan speakers, collectively known as the Dene, which simply means "people." The Sarcee of the Blackfoot confederacy in southern Alberta speak Athapaskan, as do the far-flung Navajo and Apache of the American southwest. The Dene are wanderers, but no matter how far they travel or how thoroughly they appear to absorb the cultures of those around them, they stubbornly maintain their Athapaskan tongue.

In the subarctic their societies were modest and mobile—modest in the sense that they weren't overtly expansionist; they were anything but simple. The basic unit was the family. The nomadic band was made up of several families bound by kinship and marriage. Sometimes they congregated in larger groups for the caribou hunt, or if the fishing was particularly good, but they were not organized politically as Europeans would understand the term. Flexibility and personal autonomy are at the core of the Dene culture. Communal or societal names reflect linguistic differences, and serve the purpose of the bureaucrat more than the Native.

Throughout the nineteenth century and well into the twentieth, the Dene depended on the fur trade for their lifestyle and their livelihood. The "mutual dependency between Indian and European" mentioned by Van Kirk proved easier for the European than the Indian to break free of.

Without the resources and technology available to the European, the Dene became victims of an image that was partly imposed and partly self-created. The anthropologist Alan D. McMillan has pointed out that it was the "complex of rifles, dog teams, trap lines and a market economy that became the 'traditional' Athapaskan culture" in the minds of Euro-Canadian society and successive local and national governments.

In the same manner, the mounted warrior with his rifle and headdress has come to epitomize the aristocracy of the plains. "In sheer artistry of dress," wrote Dickason, "the mounted plainsman achieved an elegance never surpassed; as an expression of the migratory buffalo-hunting way of life, he was his own *pièce de résistance.*" Yet this image represents—and

The image of the mounted warrior bore little resemblance to the original lifestyle of the plains cultures. *(Left to right):* Many Shots, White Headed Chief, Blackfoot scouts. *Provincial Archives of Alberta P.96*

represents only partially—perhaps 150 years in the life of that culture. The image died with the disappearance of the buffalo, and it died in agony, as Joseph Howard wrote:

> It was a tortured time—a time of war, famine, disease, moral dissolution. It was a time when smallpox, whiskey, prostitution and the slaughter of the buffalo did more to win an empire than bullets could; and perhaps the bullets could never have done it alone.

Native communities across the west are grappling with the future as they try to understand the past. Some are doing better than others. Alcohol abuse, poverty, disease, crime, family violence: for some, this is the legacy of the past three hundred years. Still, those years are barely a paragraph in the story of a people who go back twelve millennia on this continent.

The story isn't over yet.

The Assiniboine

T HE ASSINIBOINE are first mentioned in European accounts in the *Jesuit Relations* for 1640. In these voluminous documents, compiled over four decades by missionaries of the Society of Jesus, they appear first as *Assinipour*. Later, in 1657, they are referred to as *Assinipoualak*, "warriors of the rock." A less colourful tradition asserts that their name originated from an Ojibwa word meaning "the people that cook with hot stones," referring to their method of boiling water. In Alberta they became known as the Stoney, and were described by Alexander Henry the Younger as "most hospitable to strangers who arrive in their camp." Henry, a trader with the North West Company, also admired their prowess in the hunt. "It is supposed," he wrote, "that these people are the most expert and dexterous nation of the plains in constructing pounds and in driving buffalo into them."

The Assiniboine had been part of a Siouan-speaking nation that occupied the woodlands of Minnesota. Following an internal dispute, they split from the parent society and moved north, entering what is now Canada between 1600 and 1650. In the mid-seventeenth century the great majority of them were still a woodland people, occupying territory around Lake Winnipeg and Lake of the Woods in present-day Manitoba.

At that time, they were already playing a pivotal role in the fur trade. As the trade moved west, they moved with it. One branch of the community remained close to the edge of the boreal forest northwest of Lake Winnipeg, where they had frequent contact with the Woodland Cree. Another branch moved out along the valley of the Assiniboine River, gradually spreading into what is now Saskatchewan and Alberta. There, allied with the Cree, they acted as intermediaries for the fur companies, trading European goods to more distant Native groups. The acquisition of horses and guns in the mid-eighteenth century not only enhanced their trading role, but caused them to abandon their woodland origins to become plains warriors and buffalo hunters, commanding a territory that stretched from the eastern plains to Blackfoot country in the west.

By all appearances, they were a typical plains nation. They certainly weren't the only people who cooked their food by dropping hot stones in water to make it boil. Like other First Nations, they followed the buffalo through the summer and dispersed into smaller bands for the winter, reuniting in the spring for the hunt and various summer festivals. They lived in conical lodges, or tipis, constructed of poles covered with buffalo hides. Northern bands hunted moose and deer in addition to buffalo, and those close to the forest also took small animals such as beaver and porcupine.

Before they acquired horses, each family kept several dogs, descendants of the only domesticated animals their ancestors had brought with them from Asia. These were not pets but functional beasts of burden. When moving camp, winter or summer, each dog would haul its travois, a device consisting of two poles lashed together at one end and placed across the shoulders of the animal. The poles, spreading apart behind, supported a frame of woven willow on which was loaded the family's possessions, including the tipi cover. The frame of the Assiniboine travois was typically circular, and the dog travois was necessarily small. It was only when they acquired horses that they were able to load more than forty or fifty pounds on each travois, enabling them to increase the size of their tipis and multiply their household goods.

Stereograph of dog travois near Fort Walsh, 1878. *Provincial Archives of Alberta A.17492*

For crossing rivers that could not be safely forded, they commonly assembled their lodge poles into a raft, which would then be loaded with people and belongings and guided across by a strong swimmer pulling on a rope. The process was repeated as many times as necessary, presumably with several swimmers spelling each other. The Assiniboine supplemented this method of crossing deep water with a bull boat, a tublike vessel reminiscent of the Irish curragh or coracle. It was an extremely unstable craft of buffalo or moose hide stretched over a willow frame and paddled from the front.

As with other peoples of the plains, whether First Nations or newly arrived Europeans, buffalo meat was a staple of the Assiniboine diet. Fresh meat was roasted on a spit or boiled for immediate consumption, or smoked and dried for later use. One method of preparing the meat was to cook it in the beast's own stomach. Immediately after butchering, the women would split open the stomach and clean it, then arrange the tough flesh in a pit or hang it like a bag inside a tipi-like structure. Water and meat would be added, and hot stones dropped in to cook it. This method had the added advantage of yielding a broth that, depending on the amount of meat cooked and the addition of other ingredients such as wild turnips and rice, could be rich and nourishing.

Because fresh meat spoiled quickly, much of it was dried soon after slaughtering. The women cut strips from the leanest parts of the animal, then slit the strips again along their length until they resembled coarse netting. These were hung on racks to dry in the sun. As Ochankugahe, or Dan Kennedy, explained in *Recollections of an Assiniboine Chief*, "The sliced meat was turned over each day until it dried into jerk meat and was then packed away in parfleches. These parfleches were made from flint hides with the hair scraped off." Reconstituted in warm water or eaten as is, jerky was as large a part of the Native diet as was fresh meat.

Assiniboine women were also noted for their production of pemmican—from the Cree *pimikan*, aptly translated as "manufactured grease"—which was much in demand at fur trading posts. It was generally made from buffalo meat, although antelope, deer, elk, and moose were also used. Dried meat was reduced to powder by pounding it between two stones. Over this was poured a quantity of rendered fat. Often saskatoon berries or choke cherries were added, or wild peppermint leaves. The whole was mixed together, then stored in skin bags where it would keep indefinitely. Pemmican was portable and highly nutritious; one kilogram of it was equal in food value to five kilograms of fresh meat.

Indian woman making pemmican—a mixture of dried meat, fat, and berries. This nourishing mixture could be fried, boiled in a soup, or eaten as is. *Glenbow-Alberta Institute NA-879-5*

The Assiniboine depended on hunting, but they also gathered wild rice and vegetables in season, as well as saskatoon berries to supplement their diet. Dan Kennedy recalled that "the season of berry picking was always the happiest for the children. We gorged ourselves to our hearts content . . . punctuated, of course, with stomach aches." Bears were as fond of berries as the children were, however, so men stood guard as the pickers worked. The women picked the fruit and set it to dry immediately. When cured, the berries were packed in the tanned hides of buffalo calves. "When these were filled to capacity and sewed up," according to Kennedy, "they resembled large teddy bears."

Assiniboine women were skilled in assuring that no part of the buffalo went to waste. The bladder, washed and cured, was used as a container for rendered fat. The rind of the stomach was peeled off and fashioned into water bags. Sinew, cut from either side of the spine between the shoulder and the rump, was used for sewing before thread became available from European traders. The horns were boiled to make them soft, then carved into household utensils such as spoons, ladles, and combs. The cooked tongue was a particular delicacy, while the liver, kidneys, and rennet were consumed raw.

Men and women alike adorned themselves with quillwork, and later beads, fashioned into exquisite geometrical designs by the women of the band. They also wore perfume, according to Dan Kennedy, "concocted from scented herbs and barks of trees," and painted their faces with red powder: "Our toilet was incomplete without a liberal application of this red powder on our faces. Our young men and maidens were just as fastidious in these matters as the young people of today."

The Assiniboine honoured the spirits of the thunder and the sun, and they observed the chief festivals of the plains, such as the Sun Dance and the horse dance festivals held every summer. But on the whole they tended to place less reliance on such ceremonials than they did on individual visions.

Visions were brought on by fasting and supplication, which were practised by women and men alike. Contemporary European accounts refer to them as "dreamers," but the word is both inaccurate and inadequate. What the Assiniboine induced by fasting and supplication was neither hallucination nor dream, but another way of seeing the world, a heightened perception in which the forces of creation were seen to be in balance or out of balance—and, if out of balance, a means of correction might be suggested.

The Sun Dance was the greatest communal event of all the seasons. "They often speak of it in the course of the year," wrote Pierre de Smet, a Jesuit missionary, "and look forward to its immediate arrival with joy, respect, and veneration." After a successful hunt to ensure enough meat for the festival, the people moved to a previously chosen site. From there the hunters would go forth in search of a suitable tree to use as the centre post of the Sun Dance lodge. Once found, it would be approached as if it were an enemy, the warriors stalking it and counting coup on it before cutting it down and dragging it into camp, where they were greeted amid general rejoicing. The lodge would then be built, and people would tie their offerings to the pole and the rafters as the leader of the festival offered prayers.

The ceremonies lasted three days. The first day was for ritual dancing. On the second, the medicine men demonstrated their skills. The third was given over to feasting. It was a simpler festival than that observed by other plains peoples, with fewer rituals and taboos, and no spiritual discipline as practised by the Blackfoot.

Aside from the festivals and dances, day-to-day customs were observed, some varying from band to band but many practised by all. At the naming ceremony, for instance, an elder warrior would hold the infant and name it according to a vision he had experienced or a feat he had performed in battle. Relatives and friends would then embrace the child and give it their blessing. The simplicity of the ritual, however, was no measure of its importance, for in a child's name could be embodied both the tradition of the people and the history of the child's family.

Marriage, too, was a deceptively simple affair. At one time a suitor simply made his offer through an elder of the band and, if her parents approved the bride price, the girl moved over to his dwelling that night. By the mid-nineteenth century, perhaps due to the influence of missionaries, a ceremony had evolved that included the bearing of gifts in formal procession between the tipis of the respective parents of the bride and the groom.

Funerals were more obviously elaborate. Occasionally, as Henry Kelsey reported, a body was cremated: "This morning his body was burned according to their way, they making a great feast for him." After the flesh had been consumed in the flames, "his Bones were taken and buried with Loggs set up round of about ten feet Long."

Sometimes warriors were buried with their weapons and shield and various ceremonial objects, and the band would erect a cairn of stones or wood over the grave. Pierre de Smet recorded the most common procedure in his *Life and Travels Among the North American Indians*:

> They bind the bodies with thongs of rawhide between the branches of large trees, and, more frequently, place them on scaffolds, to protect them from the wolves and other wild animals . . . The feet are always turned to the west. There they are left to decay. When the scaffolds or the trees to which the dead are attached fall, through old age, the relatives bury all the other bones, and place the skulls in a circle on the plain, with the faces turned toward the centre. They preserve these with care, and consider them objects of religious veneration. You will generally find there several bison skulls. In the centre stands the

Assiniboine council near Fort Walsh, 1878. *Glenbow-Alberta Institute NA–936–34*

medicine pole . . . to guard and protect the sacred deposit. The Indians call the cemetery *the village of the dead*. They visit it at certain seasons of the year, to converse affectionately with their deceased relatives and friends, and always leave some present.

The Assiniboine had no hereditary class of chieftains or nobles. The only way a man could gain honour and rank was to prove himself worthy of it in bravery and battle. Such a man might be chosen as chief by the elders and the warriors, but he ruled only according to the respect or fear he inspired in them. When several bands came together, a single chief would dominate, but again, his rank was more symbolic than real. It was the military society, composed of active men between the ages of twenty-five and thirty-five, that really controlled each camp. The chief could only implement his objectives if they happened to coincide with the wishes of the military society and its leadership. These warriors were the policemen of the camp, enforcing customs and laws, authorizing raids for horses and scalps, receiving delegations from other bands, and regulating the buffalo hunt. This latter was of primary importance, for the culture and well-being of the race was dependent on this migratory animal.

"They first choose a band of warriors to hinder the hunters from leaving camp," wrote Father de Smet, "either alone or in detached companies, lest the bisons be disturbed, and thus be driven away from the encampment." The law was rigid. It applied not only to members of the camp but also to passing travellers, even those who might know nothing of the contemplated hunt. In Assiniboine society, ignorance of the law was no excuse. Some leniency might be shown to outsiders, but for members of the camp who challenged or violated the rule of the military society, the penalties could be severe:

> Their guns, their bows, and arrows are broken, their lodges cut in pieces, their dogs killed, all their provisions and their hides are taken from them. If they are bold enough to resist this penalty, they are beaten with bows, sticks, and clubs, and this torment frequently terminates in the death of the unhappy transgressor.

In the days before the horse, contact with hostile bands was sporadic. Like all plains warriors, the Assiniboine made use of the bow and arrow, with stone-headed clubs and long-handled spears for close fighting. They wore jackets of quilted moose leather for protection, and a notable warrior might have a shield of buffalo hide painted with his vision symbols. A few warriors had special skin shirts and war bonnets; the right to wear them could be granted only through a vision, although they could be bought from a warrior who had himself received permission in a vision.

A warrior who dreamed of killing an enemy regarded it as a prophecy. He would raise a band of volunteers and, with the permission of the military society, set forth to capture scalps and horses. Tipi paintings illustrated his exploits, and the eagle feathers in his headdress recorded the number of enemies he had slain. If he returned to camp victorious, the women would dance around the captured scalps in celebration, and the elders would recount their own exploits, passing their history on to the young.

Horses and firearms gave the same stimulus to war that they gave to the buffalo hunt. Distances that had been insurmountable on foot were easily covered on horseback, and no one really slept easily on the plains

Drawings on tipi of Twoyoungman, Assiniboine (Stoney) Indian, shows a great buffalo hunter, who could kill with bow and arrow. *Glenbow-Alberta Institute NA-841-511*

after 1750. The Assiniboine spent the better part of a century waging intermittent war against the Blackfoot confederacy to the west, their own kin the Sioux and other First Nations to the south, and even the Kootenay and Salish across the mountains.

It was the bands of Assiniboine who wrested the foothills and the eastern slopes of the Rockies from the Blackfoot, or Siksikah, that became known as the Stoney. Separated from their allies and kin, they held the territory alone, hunting buffalo on the plains and elk in the mountains, and trading furs, hides, and meat at Rocky Mountain House and Fort Edmonton. They were highly regarded as guides by explorers, surveyors, and missionaries, and were one of the few plains nations to respond with any enthusiasm to the message of Christianity. They too, however, lived in a more or less perpetual state of warfare, raiding the Siksikah and being raided in turn.

There are no reliable estimates of the Assiniboine population before the nineteenth century. From 1800 to 1825 it fluctuated between eight thousand and ten thousand across sixteen or seventeen bands. Continual warfare took its toll, however, along with smallpox and other diseases. At least half the population perished in one epidemic in the late 1830s, drastically reducing their importance in the fur trade. By 1860 they were greatly reduced in numbers and territory, and would doubtless have been wiped out entirely had not their enemies been suffering the same tragedies and privations.

Alcohol, too, took its toll as unscrupulous traders sought quick profits by enslaving an unsuspecting people to an unknown and highly addictive drug. In exchange for valuable furs, meat, and pemmican, Natives received a few pints of raw alcohol diluted three-to-one with water and flavoured with tea or chewing tobacco, ginger, and a few red peppers. "I never knowed what made an Injun so crazy when he drunk till I tried this booze," remarked Charles M. Russell, a cowboy artist from Montana. He went on to describe a drinking party with a camp of Assiniboine, where the first thing he noticed was the women hiding the weapons. Luckily, the white men had left their weapons in their own camp, for within an hour they were all "so disagreeable that a shepherd dog couldn't have got along with us." The whisky "sure was a brave-maker," Russell concluded; you could "shoot a man through the brain or heart and he wouldn't die till he sobered up." By the end of the evening the cowboys had become so obnoxious that the Assiniboine moved camp.

With the disappearance of the buffalo and the influx of European settlers, they were forced to submit to confinement on reserves. Those who

Stoney children at residential school, 1901. *Glenbow-Alberta Institute NA–1913–7*

lived south of the forty-ninth parallel had signed the Judith River Treaty in 1855 and now occupy reservations in the United States. The Stoney in Alberta, who had lived long enough apart from the parent society to develop differences in language and culture, signed Treaty #7 at Blackfoot Crossing in 1877, and today occupy five reserves in that province. They still hunt and trap and act as guides for hunters, but have expanded their activities to include ranching, lumbering, and the manufacture and sale of handicrafts. The bands at Morley also enjoy a substantial income from natural gas royalties, and operate commercial enterprises such as restaurants, service stations, and tourist facilities.

The rest, signators to Treaty #4 in 1874 and Treaty #6 in 1876, occupy three reserves in Saskatchewan, one of which they share with Saulteaux and Cree. Although nowhere near their population levels in the first quarter of the nineteenth century, they have recovered to nearly forty-five hundred, including the Stoney, in the last quarter of the twentieth.

The Blackfoot Confederacy

⋯⋯⋯⋯⋯

T HE BLACKFOOT CONFEDERACY was made up of five distinct nations, commonly known as the Blackfoot, the Blood, the Peigan, the Sarcee, and the Gros Ventre. The first three, collectively known as the Blackfoot, share a common language and culture. Various writers have tried to distinguish between the society known as the Blackfoot and the larger collectivity that includes the three nations of the Blackfoot, the Blood, and the Peigan. It is impossible to do so without referring to the smaller group as the "Blackfoot Proper," as if there were something improper about the others, or the "Blackfoot Tribe." The word "tribe" has a pejorative connotation, and many First Nations people now reject it, although sometimes its use is unavoidable. For the sake not only of clarity but of respect for Native preferences, then, the term "Blackfoot" will be used to denote the three nations, while "Siksikah" will be used instead of "Blackfoot Proper" or "Blackfoot Tribe" to distinguish the smaller society from the larger group.

The Nations of the Blackfoot

T HE NAMES by which many First Nations are known today, in English or French, often bear little resemblance to the names by which they know themselves. In their own Algonquian language, the Blackfoot are called *Soyitapi*, "prairie people." There are three distinct nations, each with its own chiefs and its own councils: the Siksikah, the Blood, and the Peigan. The single term "Blackfoot" to describe all three was something of a liberty taken by the fur traders who first came into contact with them in the mid-1700s.

The Peigan are the southernmost nation of the Blackfoot, and the most populous. Contradictory traditions make it impossible to determine the real significance of their name, but a Blackfoot legend claims that a traveller from the north found the people wearing skins that still had bits of meat and hair clinging to them. The women of the community had become lazy, he concluded, so he called them *Apikuni*, which means "scabby hides" or "poorly dressed robes," and the word eventually evolved to "Peigan."

The same traveller, visiting the Blood, wished to meet with the chief, but everyone he spoke to claimed to hold that rank. So he called them *Akainai*, "many chiefs," from which comes *Kainai*, the name by which they know themselves. The appellation "Blood" was imparted by the Cree, who referred to them as "red people" because of the ochre they spread on their clothes. This was later translated as "blood people" or simply "blood." It was the many chiefs of the Blood who noticed that the traveller's moccasins had been stained by ash from a prairie fire, so they called him *Siksikah*, Blackfoot.

One suspects the story was concocted by the Assiniboine or the Dakota, as it presents the three nations of the Blackfoot in a rather poor light, what with their dirty feet, their scabby hides, and their collective delusion about chieftainship—either that or the Blackfoot had such a strong

Blood encampment, south of Fort Macleod, 1883–84. *Provincial Archives of Alberta A.18697*

The Blackfoot nation and the Crow were long-time enemies. This photo, taken by a member of the British North American Boundary Survey in 1873, shows the remains of Crow Indians who were killed in battle by the Peigan in the Sweetgrass Hills. *Provincial Archives of Manitoba Boundary Commission 181 N11942*

sense of themselves and their place in the world that they were able to indulge that most admirable of human traits, a sense of humour.

The nations of the Blackfoot were sometimes at odds with one another, but a common language and customs and frequent intermarriage were proof against open warfare. Besides, it was crucial that they present a united front to their enemies, who were legion: the Kootenay and Salish to the west; the Crow, Shoshoni, Nez Percé, and Dakota to the south; and the Plains Cree and Assiniboine to the north and east. By 1800 they had permanently driven the Shoshoni from what was to become the Canadian plains, although they remained a preferred enemy for decades. The Crow, too, had been driven out in the late 1700s, but they continued to make war against the Blackfoot into the 1880s.

At the height of their power, the Blackfoot commanded territory from the North Saskatchewan River south to the Missouri, and from the present Alberta-Saskatchewan border to the Rocky Mountains. They hunted on the high plains and in the foothills. They took elk on the lower slopes of the Rockies, and occasionally mountain goats and sheep. They snared deer and smaller game, but the buffalo alone was *nitapiksisako*, "real meat." Everything else was inferior. When the Hudson's Bay Company sent Anthony Henday to persuade the western nations to bring their furs to York Factory on Hudson Bay, the Blackfoot declined. It was too far, they said; they couldn't live that long without real meat.

Henday travelled farther into western Canada than any European before him, but when he arrived among the Blackfoot in 1754 he found them already well supplied with axes, beads, guns, hatchets, knives, and pots. Some of these, originating from trading posts on Hudson Bay the previous century, had been traded from band to band across parkland and plain. Others had been bartered for horses, buffalo robes, and dried meat by the Cree and the Assiniboine, who acted as intermediaries for the traders.

Because they spoke the Algonquian language of eastern Canada, early explorers and later historians concluded that the Blackfoot, like the Cree, had once been a woodland people, and it was only with the acquisition of horses and firearms that they were able to push westward to occupy the high plains east of the Rockies. The Blackfoot, for their part, scorned the idea that they had come from the east. The great chief Crowfoot of the Siksikah knew of no tradition among the three nations that would lead anyone to believe they had ever lived anywhere but on the high plains. According to the Peigan creation myth, this was the island the Old Man had created for them, and the existence of the Oldman River in Peigan territory was witness to that ancient tradition. As evidence of their origins, it was at least as compelling as their language.

Whatever the truth of it, there can be no doubt that, of all the First Nations living on the Canadian plains at the time of European contact, none but the Blackfoot had any claim to antiquity there. If they had once been a woodland nation, they had long since divested themselves of any trace of woodland culture.

Like their allies and their enemies, the Blackfoot lived in tipis and roamed the prairie in seasonal patterns following the buffalo herds. Their clothing was typical of plains societies: shirt, breech cloth, leggings, and moccasins, a costume "at once simple and commodious," according to Alexander Macken-zie. They used a travois to transport their household possessions. They paid honour to the thunder and the sun, whose spirits were so apparent and dramatic in the natural world. They used clay vessels and hot stones to cook their food, but later switched back to the earlier vessels of hide because it was a thankless task to transport pottery by horse travois.

Women were highly regarded, and played a central role in important ceremonies. They were expected to be faithful, generous, hospitable, industrious, and skilled in the arts. They were also expected to show courage when the occasion demanded it, and rarely failed to match or exceed the boldness of their male counterparts. In 1870, when a party of raiding Cree fell upon a small Blackfoot camp at Many Ghosts on the Oldman River, one woman killed four of the attackers while others of the camp swam the river to summon aid. She was armed with only a tomahawk, and her name is lost to history.

While women were only occasionally expected to take part in battle, the arts were virtually their exclusive domain. It was believed that the Thunder Spirit had given the porcupine to the Blackfoot, and taught them how to dye the creature's quills and work them into intricate and beautiful patterns. Quill workers' societies were limited to a few select women who had mastered the skills and techniques of this demanding craft.

Prayer and ritual were essential accompaniments to the work. The quill worker would paint her hands and face to protect against blindness and the swelling that could result from the prick of a barbed quill. She would wear a certain amulet or necklace to signify to others that she was practising the sacred craft and should not be distracted. By painstaking techniques of wrapping, plaiting, sewing, and weaving the brightly coloured quills, she turned the functional objects of everyday life into works of art. Shirts and pipe stems, pouches and armbands, breastplates and moccasins, knife sheaths and cradle boards: all were transformed in her hands. When she became too old to continue, a younger woman, preferably a relative, would be initiated into the society by the elder who was leaving. The initiate's first work would be offered to the sun.

The women owned the hides and the tipis, but the men were the heads of the household. A troublesome wife could be sent back to her family. Polygamy was common, and often occurred at the request of women so that they could share the burdens of child-bearing and household duties. As a purely practical arrangement it worked out well, for there was frequently a shortage of men owing to the casualties of war.

Like the Assiniboine, the Blackfoot usually placed their dead in trees, but they had no subsequent ceremony for the bones. Prominent men and women were sometimes laid out in their tipis, the edges weighted with stones to discourage scavengers. At funerals and in mourning, women would cut their hair as a sign of grief, and occasionally slice off the tip of a finger if the death was someone particularly dear. Men, too, followed this practice, although before the nations had been confined on

The Blackfoot generally placed their dead in trees. Pictured here is a Blood tree burial, 1800s. *Glenbow-Alberta Institute NA-1376-4*

reserves, a widower was more likely to assuage his grief by going to war.

The band was a self-contained unit, small enough to find food for all but large enough to defend itself. There was a political chief in normal times, and a war chief who assumed control in times of danger. A head chief would be chosen at the coming together of several bands or of the entire nation. There was a degree of social ranking according to wealth and privilege, but the chief was by no means automatically at the top.

As with other plains peoples, warrior societies cut across social divisions. They held annual dances, policed the camps, received delegations, authorized raiding parties, and protected the people on the move. There were ten or twelve military societies in each of the Siksikah, the Blood, and the Peigan, arranged in a type of hierarchy by age and experience. Some were open to women. Each had one or two leaders who sat on the tribal council when the bands united in the summer for the Sun Dance and other celebrations. Membership was purchased—always an important point with the Blackfoot—but a warrior could generally sell the regalia from his previous membership to buy the regalia for the next. Membership in dancing societies was also by purchase. Their purpose could be either social or religious, or a mixture of the two, but they were all marked by the formal acquisition of the ceremonial objects and songs that went along with membership.

Medicine bundles, too, were purchased. It might be a few feathers wrapped in cloth or a multitude of articles kept in a leather bag—the skull of a bird, the skin of an animal, roots and rocks, a twist of sweetgrass, a pipe for prayer and blessing, paints and other ceremonial items—but each had its ritual significance. Every object in the bag was connected to a vision or an event; each had a song that established its validity and which its owner must chant when it was brought into the light. The formal transfer of a medicine bundle from one owner to another might take days, as the

Leading chiefs of the Blackfoot nation in 1884. *(Back, left to right):* Jean L'Heureux, interpreter; Red Crow, head chief of the Bloods; and Sgt. W. Piercy, NWMP. *(Front):* Crowfoot, head chief of the Blackfoot; Sitting on an Eagle Tail, head chief of the Peigan; and Three Bulls, Crowfoot's brother. *Glenbow-Alberta Institute NA-13-1*

new owner had to master the significance and the song of all that he had purchased. A warrior might beggar himself to buy a sacred bundle, but the prestige of owning it far outweighed the host of obligations and taboos it incurred both for him and for his wife.

All plains nations shared the basic ritual of the Sun Dance, which continues in various forms down to the present day, but there have always been considerable variations among them. As Mike Mountain Horse explained in *My People the Bloods*, "The Sun Dance originated among my people long before the advent of the white race. It is an annual tribal ceremony held in the summertime to propitiate the Sun and other lesser spirits." Among the Blackfoot and the Sarcee, the festival was sponsored by a virtuous woman in response to a vow she had taken in a time of crisis, often the illness of a relative. She would announce to the camp that, in supplication to the divine powers, she would officiate at a Sun Dance the following summer, and erect the Sun Dance lodge. From that point she would begin to accumulate buffalo tongues, which would be cut into slabs and dried, "to be taken as sacred food at a great public communion celebrated during the Sun Dance." In this she was assisted by other women of unquestioned virtue. In tones reminiscent of a missionary preacher, Mountain Horse wrote: "All these women are first required to openly declare themselves as having lived an upright and chaste life. If one is found to be of questionable character, she is immediately disqualified and is not even allowed to remain in the sacred lodge."

As the sponsor of the Sun Dance fasted and prayed, the minor chiefs of the community erected the framework of the lodge, and a pair of warriors went in search of a suitable tree for the centre pole. When they found one, they marked it and returned to camp. It was then the privilege of the Horn Society, a secret organization of men and women, to fell the tree, trim and peel it, and bring it to the site of the Sun Dance lodge. This was accomplished only with great ceremony, and the pole was erected in the same manner. It was then decorated with birds, horses, buffalo, and dream images either painted or carved into the wood. Offerings were hung from the rafter poles, and an altar with a buffalo skull and sweetgrass was erected at its base. At that point the Sun Dance woman's task was over: she had fasted for four days, overseen the communion of the buffalo tongues, and supervised the erection of the lodge, which was circular, with a roof and walls of leafy branches. The dance began when it was ready.

Among the Blood when Mike Mountain Horse was a boy in the 1890s, the different lodges and societies of the community then took over the

Blackfoot medicine men beside Sun Dance lodge. *Provincial Archives of Alberta P.111*

ceremonies. These included the Horn Society, which was the senior lodge, the Eagle Society, the Black Police, the Dogs, the Flies, the Crazy Dogs, the Pigeon Society, and the Buffaloes, or women's society. Any two of these groups could preside over a day's ceremonies at a Sun Dance. As many of them were secret organizations, it is difficult to guess at their precise nature and function. The missionary Calvin McQuesten attempted to record a Pigeon Society ceremony at a Sun Dance in 1907, but what his photographs mostly record is one of the participants rushing toward him to make him stop. Mountain Horse wrote only that "their rites consist chiefly of dances."

Many of the participants, like the sponsor, danced in fulfilment of vows they had made, or in thanksgiving for blessings they had received. Often they continued without food, water, or sleep for the duration of the festival, moving in place, their gaze fixed upon the sacred centre pole. One of these might be a warrior who danced alone at the entrance to the lodge.

This was a place reserved for a man of conspicuous courage—and conspicuous wealth. As Mountain Horse explained, "Considerable payment is required of those who dance in this honoured place. Horses and goods are lavishly given away by these dancing warriors." The only value of wealth was that it could be given away; the idea of owning things out of sheer acquisitiveness was unknown.

Dancing gave way to feasting, which gave way once again to dancing. Gift giving was prominent in many celebrations, and often the elders related the oral traditions of the people while warriors reenacted skirmishes in which they had taken part. In this way history was passed from generation to generation.

Young men sometimes underwent an ancient custom that has been variously described as "voluntary torture" or "the making of a brave." With their breasts pierced with wooden skewers that were then attached by thongs to the top of the centre pole, they would dance, leaning backward against the thongs, until the skewers ripped free. Sometimes the back was pierced as well, and a buffalo skull or a heavy shield hung by thongs from the skewers until its weight ripped the flesh and set the dancer free. Occasionally others would have to cut or pull him free.

Some observers have claimed that all males had to undergo this ordeal at a certain age in order to be accepted as "braves," but in fact it was purely voluntary. It was looked on as a sacrifice to propitiate the sun when a beloved relative was gravely ill. A Blood named Eagle Ribs once underwent the ordeal three days in succession to aid the recovery of his father.

"Making a Brave"—photo taken on the Blood Reserve in 1887. *Provincial Archives of Alberta* B.990

While the Siksikah, the Blood, and the Peigan made up the Blackfoot nations, the Blackfoot confederacy also included the Sarcee to the northwest and, until 1861, the Gros Ventre to the southeast. A dispute over stolen horses in that year converted the Gros Ventre from occasional allies to implacable foes. A similar disagreement had driven a wedge between the Blackfoot and the Cree in the early 1800s, for they had enjoyed a mutually profitable alliance before that. Raiding for horses made enemies, and it was no minor activity. In 1810, Fort Edmonton alone reported the loss of 650 horses in the area.

The horse evolved in North America. The fossil record is complete, from the diminutive *eohippus* of forty million years ago to animals approaching the size and appearance of the modern horse. Horse and human coexisted for a time on this continent: bones, arrowheads, and ashes found at prehistoric campsites are persuasive evidence that humans occasionally feasted on equine flesh. By the time horses became extinct on this continent, enough had migrated to Asia by way of Beringia—for the traffic was not only one-way—to maintain the species.

It was the conquistador Hernando Cortez who, in 1519, reintroduced the horse to its native soil. From those and subsequent landings, the animal made its way steadily back across the plains of its ancestry, largely through barter and theft. By 1650 the First Nations of the American southwest had become horse cultures. Less than a century later the Blackfoot, too, had acquired *misstutin*—"big dogs"—and when Anthony Henday arrived in 1754 they were already accomplished riders.

The horse changed virtually every aspect of life on the plains. It gave the band mobility and speed. To the individual it imparted wealth and status. It was a source of pride as well as a cause and a means of war. Marriages and alliances were sealed or broken by the exchange or theft of horses. They were a measure of bravery, representing both prizes to be taken and thefts to be avenged.

Horses were a mixed blessing, however; for if the Blackfoot acquired them first, others soon followed, friend and foe alike. The same was true of firearms, which the Blackfoot obtained from Cree intermediaries at about the same time they acquired horses, in the early eighteenth century. Within a few decades the Peigan had expanded into Montana, but their northern boundary had retreated south of the Bow River. The Blood, who had occupied territory between the Red Deer and Bow Rivers, moved down to the Sweetgrass Hills and present-day Lethbridge. The Siksikah, the most northerly and numerically the smallest of the three nations, were

Blackfoot Crossing, on the Bow River, 1881. *Glenbow-Alberta Institute NA-1190-9*

also forced south under pressure from their armed and mounted neighbours, finally centring on Blackfoot Crossing and the Red Deer River.

In 1806 a member of the Lewis and Clark expedition killed a Peigan, thus setting the tone for future encounters with Americans. The Blackfoot didn't care for American trading methods, either. They were used to bartering furs, robes, and meat to the posts, but American mountain men harvested the robes and pelts themselves, bypassing the Native population entirely. The Blackfoot felt they were being robbed, and clashes with whites became common.

In 1831 the American Fur Company made peace with the Blackfoot and built Fort Piegan—the Americans transposed the "e" and the "i"—on the Missouri River. By then the North West Company and the Hudson's Bay Company had merged, so First Nations could no longer pit one against the other to get the best price. The prospect of playing the Americans against the British, however, turned the Blackfoot into keen traders, if they had not been so before.

In 1855 the United States, wanting clear title to Indian land, negotiated a treaty with the Blackfoot, who surrendered much of Montana in exchange for various benefits, including annuity payments and hunting rights. The major Peigan chiefs were signators to the treaty, but many of the Blood and most of the Siksikah lived in what was then British territory and took no interest in American domestic policy.

A steady trickle of free traders and missionaries into the newly ceded territory turned into a Caucasian flood when gold was discovered in the Rocky Mountains of southwestern Montana. Clashes between Indians and whites once again became common, to the point that Americans came to refer to the conflict as the Blackfoot War. It came to a tragic end in January 1870 when a detachment of the United States 2nd Cavalry led by Colonel Eugene Baker swept down upon a camp of peaceful Peigan on the Marias River, north of Fort Benton, killing 173 people, wounding 20 more, and burning forty-one lodges. One trooper was killed. At the subsequent inquiry, a certain Lieutenant Pease testified that 140 of the dead had been women and children; another 18 were old men. In his defence, Colonel Baker claimed that 120 of the 173 were vigorous warriors, but further evidence suggested that many in the camp had in fact been ill with smallpox. Baker's intentions, if they had ever been in doubt, were crystallized in the words of an early Montana historian who referred to the brutish slaughter as "the first great lesson in good manners taught the savage of this Territory." Many Blackfoot fled to the Canadian side of the border, for it had become clear that the United States intended to commit genocide upon them.

But even here they were not free from the evils of American enterprise. By 1870 the buffalo had virtually disappeared from the eastern prairie. There were a few herds left in the west, but the Blackfoot, too, had been devastated. Disease and starvation had carried off fully two-thirds of their people. They were under threat from commercial hide hunters competing for buffalo, and from American free traders selling whisky and other goods from posts with names such as Stand-Off, Slide-Out, and Whoop-Up. Taking advantage of the lack of law enforcement in the new dominion, they set the liquor flowing, in the words of an Oblate missionary, "as freely as the streams running from the Rocky Mountains."

Fort Whoop-Up, near present-day Lethbridge, was the most notorious of the whisky posts. A square stockade of vertical, sharpened logs, its doors, windows, and even chimneys barred with iron, it was designed to keep its occupants safe from the intoxicated rages of those they set out to debauch and enslave. Strategically placed rifle slits and a small cannon served to repel those who were undeterred by the fourteen-foot-high walls. The men inside were as savage as any caricature they might contrive of the warriors who gathered at the gate. Some were Civil War veterans, some were outlaws, some were merely vicious opportunists. Whatever their backgrounds, they shared a willingness to exploit the weakness of others by the crudest means possible.

Those who took their trade goods to Fort Whoop-Up were first invited in for a ceremonious welcome drink. The women might be offered a drink as well, and often they accepted. But, as Charles Russell's experience with the Assiniboine suggests, they were more likely to be hiding the weapons at that point. When trading began in earnest, the gates were closed and barred. The Indians would then line up at the front gate with their buffalo robes, their furs, and their pemmican, all of which the traders accepted through a narrow wicket in exchange for a few pints of liquid fire. When the items they had brought to trade were exhausted, they offered anything else they owned. Within a short time the traders would have relieved them of their property, their dignity, and their reason.

Group of Blackfoot at Fort Whoop-Up, 1881. *Provincial Archives of Alberta A.17475*

The fur trade may have brought new tools and weapons to the original inhabitants of the plains, but it also brought disease, alcohol, and poverty. Here Colin Fraser, the trader at Fort Chipewyan in the 1890s, examines his cache of furs. *National Archives of Canada C1229*

If, as sometimes happened, the liquor ran out, a murderous riot would ensue. Those who tried to storm the stockade walls would be pushed or shot off by the traders inside. If they could find their weapons, the warriors might attack the fort, and sometimes each other, in earnest. But the only thing the men inside really had to fear was fire, and an attack of flaming arrows was invariably met with the cannon.

At this point, if they could manage it, and if they had remained sober themselves, the women would try to drag their men away to sleep it off. Some died of alcohol poisoning during the night, others froze to death, and many more died of gunshot wounds. One winter, seventy of the Blood died in drunken disputes at one of the posts. Those who survived the night, however, paid their debts honourably, handing over the horse, the tipi, and whatever else the traders had not dared to collect the night before.

The Blackfoot and others who degraded themselves in this manner were not stupid people. Whisky traders caught on the open prairie were shot on sight, and the posts were sometimes under attack by Indians and other hunters who were quite sober. Even so, the lure of alcohol was not to be denied. Through twelve millennia the Natives of North America had developed not the slightest immunity to smallpox, measles, or tuberculosis. In the same manner, they had developed no resistance to alcohol.

Of course, they weren't the only ones. White men had been succumbing to the ravages of alcohol for millennia before it was ever introduced to the First Nations of North America. At Fort Whoop-Up, too, there was often as much violence within the stockade as without. One employee wrote to a friend in Montana that his partner had "got to putting on airs" so he shot him dead. "The potatoes is looking well," he added.

The coming of the North-West Mounted Police in 1874 stamped out the whisky trade. But by then the epidemics of the eighteenth century, the violence of the whisky traders, and the starvation that followed the disappearance of the buffalo had combined to demoralize and defeat what had once been the major military force of the northwest plains. In 1877 the Blackfoot nations finally submitted to confinement on reserves.

The Siksikah

The Blackfoot had not requested a treaty, as had the Cree and the Saulteaux, but they were facing the same challenges: the end of the fur trade, the near-extinction of the buffalo, and the increasing pressures of white settlement. Treaties with the new Dominion of Canada seemed the only practical means of preventing incoming settlers from crowding them off the land. Nonetheless, the nations of the confederacy were reluctant to sign anything, and looked to Crowfoot, head chief of the Siksikah, for leadership.

A Siksikah boy used his birth name only until his first war party, when a second was conferred on him by his comrades, often in sport or derision. On achieving manhood he took a name more befitting his status, but even that was subject to change if greater deeds were contemplated or achieved. Crowfoot had been born a Blood near the Belly River in 1830, but grew up Siksikah. During his lifetime he went to war nineteen times and was wounded six times. He once killed a grizzly bear, armed with only a lance. But his name was the result of another deed.

Killing an enemy was not as brave an action as simply touching him. Anyone could take the scalp of a man he had killed with a bullet or an

Crowfoot, head chief of the Blackfoot, 1887. *Glenbow-Alberta Institute NA-29-1*

arrow, but if you were close enough to touch a living enemy, you were in real danger. This was known as "counting coup."

As a teenager, Crowfoot accompanied a raiding party of Siksikah, Blood, and Peigan to Montana. Coming upon a Crow encampment, they saw a captured Peigan tipi erected in plain view. The Blackfoot attacked, and Crowfoot ran straight for the tipi. He was fired upon and hit in the arm. He fell, but got up and continued running under heavy fire until he reached his objective. He struck the tipi with his whip, then fell again. Another member of the raiding party helped him to safety and later verified his deed. It was then he took the name *Isapomuxika*—"Crow Indian's Big Foot"—the legacy of an honoured warrior who had left his name to the nation.

In 1865 he became chief of his band, and in 1870 one of the head chiefs of the Siksikah. He was eloquent in speech, and possessed the skills of a diplomat. He made peace with the Cree, and adopted a young man of that nation named Poundmaker as his foster son. In 1874 he welcomed the North-West Mounted Police, hoping that they could save his nation from destruction at the hands of the whisky traders. It was natural that both his own people and the Canadians should turn to him when it came to negotiating a treaty.

Crowfoot disliked the idea of giving up the land to see it swarming with white settlers and their herds of cattle. On the other hand, he knew the buffalo were disappearing and that his people would starve if they could not rely on the Canadians for help. Always a realist, he counselled the chiefs to accept the terms. Treaty #7 was signed by the Siksikah, the Blood, the Peigan, the Sarcee, and the Stoney in 1877. The terms included an annuity of five dollars per person, one square mile (260 hectares) of land for every five people, schools, hunting and fishing supplies, aid and education in agriculture, and protection of subsistence rights. The Siksikah accepted a reserve on the Bow River, and settled there in 1881.

Crowfoot counselled against participation in the North-West Rebellion of 1885, but it was hardly necessary. The Blackfoot confederacy, weakened by disease and hunger, were well acquainted with the power of the white man, and showed little inclination to take up arms against him. Crowfoot himself spent the last decade of his life mourning his children as they succumbed to tuberculosis and other diseases. The great chief died near Blackfoot Crossing in 1890.

By the turn of the century the Siksikah were farming and gardening, ranching, and mining coal on their own land. Anglican and Roman Catholic missionaries had opened day schools, and the people were being pressured to sell portions of their unused land. In 1912, the sale of 61,000 acres (24,700 hectares) generated slightly less than a million dollars for the reserve. In 1918 the sale of another 55,000 acres (22,275 hectares) brought in nearly 1.3 million dollars.

The Siksikah were suddenly the wealthiest First Nation in Canada. They built houses and roads, bought farming equipment, erected a hospital, and undertook to provide weekly rations to the entire reserve. After World War II, rapid increases in the cost of living quickly depleted reserve funds. In addition, owing to improvements in health care and nutrition, the population doubled within two decades. While this was joyous news to a people that had once feared for their existence, the strain it put on their communal resources led to the head chief announcing in

1958 that they had run out of money. The time had come, he said, for the Siksikah either to get up out of their chairs "or go to sleep altogether."

Tribally funded programs came to an end. But a tribal council now administers much of the reserve, with a native staff of teachers, social workers, counsellors, labour crews, and office personnel. A junior college, a trade school, and a cultural centre have been developed, and the population continues to expand—from eight hundred in 1939 to nearly four thousand today. Overcrowding is a problem, with its attendant problems of alcohol abuse, crime, poverty, and disease. There are no easy solutions, but the Siksikah are certainly not asleep.

The Blood

For some days in the autumn of 1877 it was feared that the Blood would not sign Treaty #7, for when the Siksikah and the Sarcee gathered at Blackfoot Crossing on the Bow River, with their traditional enemies the Stoney camped on the opposite bank, there were few Peigan in attendance, and the only Blood chief present was Medicine Calf, a man noted for his distrust of the white race. With a population of over two thousand, the Blood were the largest First Nation in the area, and their cooperation was essential if the treaty were to have any meaning. But the Blood were angry with the government and with their relatives the Siksikah.

Treaty negotiations had originally been scheduled for Fort Macleod, but Crowfoot was reluctant to decide the fate of his people inside a white man's fort. Blackfoot Crossing was chosen as an alternative, but it was in Siksikah territory and inconvenient to the Blood and the Peigan. The government refused to move the site again, with the result that a large force of agitated and apprehensive Siksikah, Sarcee, and Stoney were left to amuse themselves for two days while the Blood decided if they were going to come or not.

Eventually they did come; they did sign. And Red Crow, their eloquent chief, a renowned warrior and statesman, paid a moving tribute to Stamixotokon—"Buffalo Bull's Head," from the image of a buffalo's head on the insignia of his uniform—otherwise known as James F. Macleod, commissioner of the North-West Mounted Police. "Stamixotokon . . . has made me many promises," Red Crow declared. "He kept them all—not one of them was ever broken. Everything that the police have done has been good. I trust Stamixotokon, and will leave everything to him."

Red Crow, chief of the Blood tribe, 1895. *Glenbow-Alberta Institute NA-56-1*

Macleod had managed in three months to shut down the illegal trade in whisky that had been going on under the noses of American authorities for ten years. Even Medicine Calf was moved to pay tribute. "I can sleep now safely," he said. "Before the arrival of the Police, when I laid my head down at night, every sound frightened me; my sleep was broken; now I can sleep sound and I am not afraid."

In 1878 a prairie fire drove what was left of the buffalo into Montana. The following spring the entire Blood nation followed them down for the last great hunt. Then the buffalo disappeared. The elders speculated that the Great Spirit had driven them into the earth as punishment for signing the treaty. The government had thought the herds would last another

decade, so they were not prepared as the Blood, starving and confused, made their way home.

Originally they were given a reserve next to the Siksikah on the Bow River, where the reality of reserve life led more than a few of them to the conclusion that signing the treaty had not been such a good idea after all. It was a miserable strip of land, dull and dry. They voiced their discontent, and authorities allowed them to move onto a site between the St. Mary and Belly Rivers, their traditional winter camping grounds. When a new treaty was signed in 1883 it became the largest reserve in Canada.

Already in 1881 they had started breaking land, and in 1882 they produced enormous crops of potatoes and turnips. To the surprise of many, including the Canadian government, the warlike Blood had become excellent farmers. In his report for 1882, however, the commissioner of the North-West Mounted Police pointed out that it was not a good idea to allow them "to leave their reserve in large numbers." For they hadn't given up their old ways entirely. When they weren't farming, apparently, they were mounting horse-raiding expeditions to the United States, for which they could not be prosecuted as long as they managed to make it back to Canada without being caught.

Mission on Blood Reserve, south of Fort Macleod, 1885. *Provincial Archives of Alberta A.18688*

Red Crow encouraged self-sufficiency and education. He introduced ranching to the Blood, at the same time urging them to retain their customs and religion. By the time of his death in 1900 they were a self-assured, confident people who considered themselves the equal of any white man.

Today, the Blood reserve is administered by a chief and council. They publish a newspaper, manufacture prefabricated homes, and operate a supermarket, among other commercial enterprises. They are farmers and ranchers, also artists, teachers, and professionals. In the words of Hugh Dempsey, the compassionate chronicler of Indian life in Alberta, they have become "one of the most progressive tribes in Canada."

The Peigan

The Peigan in southern Alberta are what is left of the most populous nation of the Blackfoot. They had divided into the North and South Peigan in the middle of the nineteenth century, and at the signing of Treaty #7 their respective populations were 720 and 3,240. Only the smaller North Peigan were signators, however, as a previous agreement with the United States had been signed in 1855 and the South Peigan were already settled on a reservation in Montana. The latter now call themselves the Blackfeet Indians of Montana, and the North Peigan are known simply as the Peigan.

On signing Treaty #7 in 1877, the Peigan requested a reserve on their winter hunting grounds, "on the Old Man's river, near the foot of the Porcupine Hills, at a place called Crow's Creek," where the government proceeded to implement its policy of turning the Natives into farmers. The

Peigan were willing enough—the alternatives were few—and in the first few years enjoyed some notable successes. In 1881 an inspector was able to report that the Peigan were "very well-to-do and will, in my opinion, be the first of the Southern Plains Indians to become self-supporting."

The inspector had little sense of history, for the Peigan had been self-supporting for thousands of years before European contact. A series of droughts and insect infestations proved him wrong about their farming operations, too. But it was government policy that Indians should be farmers, so the Peigan continued to farm. In 1894 the agent on the reserve reported that "no grain will mature properly in this location," but the Peigan were told to continue farming. In 1898 the agent stated flatly, "Climatic conditions of wind, drought, and frost prohibit successful farming on this reserve." He noted somewhat patronizingly that, "While the preparation of the ground was a wholesome—though discouraging—occupation for the Indians, the seed grain was literally thrown away . . . "

The first few crops had been a fluke. The Peigan were not successful farmers; they were disillusioned Indians, and close to despair. Adding to their misery were the white man's diseases. Scrofula and tuberculosis were particularly virulent, and the influenza epidemic of 1918 reduced their numbers to 250.

Even so, they retained their language, their religion, and many of their customs. The Sun Dance was celebrated annually, despite official efforts to suppress it. They raised cattle and horses, and built a sawmill with the

Government policy attempted to turn Natives into farmers. This photo of a threshing outfit was taken at Dunbow (St. Joseph's) Industrial School, DeWinton, AB, 1920s. *Provincial Archives of Alberta OB.8795*

Students at boarding school, Peigan Reserve, Brocket, AB, ca. 1900. *Provincial Archives of Alberta OB.8900*

proceeds from selling the right-of-way to the railroad that cut through the centre of the reserve in 1899. Eventually, new varieties of seed grain allowed them to begin farming again with some prospect of success.

Native successes, however, were viewed with disfavour by encroaching white settlers. Euro-Canadian farmers regarded the Indians as subsidized competition, and they made their views known to politicians. As permits were required to sell produce, it was a relatively easy thing for Department of Indian Affairs officials to prevent bands from selling their produce at local markets. With no profit from their farming operations, there were no funds for expansion, or for buying new machinery. Nor could the Peigan or any other nation borrow money to buy equipment, as the Indian Act forbade the mortgaging of reserve lands. This was part of official policy to keep the Natives at a subsistence level of farming. If they began farming on a large scale with complicated machinery, it was feared, there would be no one to service the machinery once the farm instructors left.

The Peigan managed to rise above this philosophy by diversifying their operations. After World War II, health and educational services improved. The Peigan assumed the administration of their reserve, and were among the first aboriginal people in Canada to demand a vote in provincial elections. They developed a ranching enterprise, a garment factory, and an operation that mass produces moccasins for sale. From near-extinction in 1918, the population on the reserve now exceeds two thousand.

The Sarcee

IN THE ATHAPASKAN TONGUE, the Sarcee are *tsotli'na* or "earth people," according to one source. According to another, they are *tsúùt'ína* or "many people." How they came to be called Sarcee is also obscure. A tradition within the Sarcee maintains that they used to be called *Saxsiiwak*, "strong people," which evolved to "Sarcee" over the years. It has also been suggested that the name comes from two Blackfoot words, *sa* and *ahksi*, meaning "no" and "good." As Hugh Dempsey has pointed out, however, the proper term for "no good" in the Blackfoot tongue is *matsokapi*, not *sahksi*. Perhaps the problem is, as the trader Alexander Henry said, that the Athapaskan language is "so difficult to acquire that none of our people have ever learned it."

The origins of the Sarcee are marginally less obscure. The Anglican priest H.W. Gibbon Stocken, who lived among the Blackfoot and the Sarcee, wrote with the certitude typical of his generation: "The Sarcee are a portion of the Beaver tribe who lived along the great Mackenzie River. Internal feuds were always breaking out amongst them, and at last our portion was driven south, never to return." According to another story, the people were crossing a frozen river when the ice broke. Those who had already crossed became the Sarcee; those who remained behind became the Beaver. In a more poetic version, the people were crossing a frozen lake when a woman saw a horn protruding from the ice. She grasped it and tried to pull it free, whereupon the earth shook and the ice groaned and a great crack appeared, dividing the lake in two. Part of the group fled north, while the rest fled south. The northern portion returned to the traditional hunting grounds of the Beaver. The southern part kept moving until they reached the plains, where they became the Sarcee.

Sarcee tradition does recount a common origin with the Beaver of the subarctic, and anthropological evidence bears it out. But here again historians are not entirely in agreement. One theory has the Sarcee being separated from the parent nation and driven south by the encroaching Cree in the mid-eighteenth century. If this was the case, they would have been venturing onto the plains not long before fur traders first encountered them in the late eighteenth century. Another theory has the Sarcee established on the plains long before Europeans arrived. Matthew Cocking, exploring westward for the Hudson's Bay Company in 1772-73, found them a distinct group of "Equestrian Indians,"

Sarcee Indians in southern Alberta, 1887–88. *Provincial Archives of Alberta B.37*

which they likely would not have been had they arrived only recently.

The anthropologist Diamond Jenness spent two months among the Sarcee in the early 1920s, learning the traditional life of the people from the elders. He described them as the remnant of a once-powerful nation that had moved down from the north some centuries ago. "Though assimilated to the Blackfoot in all their customs," he wrote, "they still preserve their Athapaskan tongue." He felt sure they would not have survived on the prairies had it not been for their alliance with the Blackfoot, and in fact considered them in most things a weak reflection of their allies.

By contrast, Alexander Henry's description of the Sarcee little more than a century earlier paid them high honour by his own European standards:

> These people have the reputation of being the bravest tribe in all the plains, who dare face ten times their own numbers, and of this I have had convincing proof during my residence in this country. They are more civilized and more closely attached to us than the [Blackfoot], and have on several occasions offered to fight the others in our defence. None of their neighbours can injure them with impunity . . .

In the early nineteenth century David Thompson reported their population to be in the neighbourhood of 650. Scarcely fifty years later John Palliser placed it at 1,400. Their territory ranged from the Peace River in the north to the Red Deer River in the south. They appeared to have been allied more closely with the Siksikah than with the Blood or the Peigan. This was certainly the case at the signing of Treaty #7 in 1877, when the Siksikah and the Sarcee, with their traditional enemies the Stoney, waited two days for the Blood and the Peigan to show up in sufficient numbers to lend credence to their signing.

The Sarcee, like the nations of the Blackfoot, were divided into bands and military societies. They observed the same rituals for marriages, funerals, the Sun Dance, and other festivals. They painted their faces, sometimes covering the entire upper half with ochre or vermilion, like a mask. Warfare was a passion with them, as it was with their enemies, sometimes lasting generations as each side sought to avenge previous losses and gain prestige. The Sarcee fasted and feasted, danced and prayed, purified themselves in the sweat lodge, and generally shared all things but their language with the Blackfoot.

Buffalo meat was the foundation of the Sarcee diet, although elk and deer were also available in the foothills and the parklands, and fleet pronghorns were plentiful all across the prairie. The wild turnip was an important vegetable; it was eaten raw, roasted, boiled, or pounded into a kind of flour and added to other dishes. The learned women of the community also collected wild herbs and plants for medicinal use.

But in the end it was the buffalo that fed them and defined them, and in this they followed not only the Blackfoot but every other plains culture. As long as the herds lasted, they held their own—despite the warfare, the raiding for horses and scalps, despite the interference of an alien culture, despite even the diseases the Europeans brought among them. As long as the herds lasted, there was one part of them that could survive, adapt, even thrive, achieving new heights of cultural expression. But it was the disappearance of the herds that they could not accommodate. Their culture had been based on the buffalo, and suddenly the buffalo were no more.

At the signing of Treaty #7, the Sarcee were to share a reserve with the Siksikah and the Blood on the Bow River. They paid no attention, and resumed their nomadic life. In 1878 they managed to kill enough buffalo to stay alive, but if they were to supplement this meagre diet with rations from the government they would have to move onto their reserve. The following year they did, but they quarrelled with the Siksikah and soon

Sweatlodge frame for the Sarcee Sun Dance, 1911. The buffalo skull served as an altar piece. The paddle at the right was used for carrying hot stones for the ritual. *Glenbow-Alberta Institute NB-16-568*

moved away again. Many followed the last herds into Montana, but in 1880 they were forced to return home to government rations of beef and flour.

They soon quarrelled with the Siksikah again, and when their rations ran out they moved to Calgary, where their head chief, aptly named Bull Head, was determined to stay. The three-man police detachment grew alarmed when a band of Sarcee tried to burn down a trading post, and an Indian agent was dispatched to speak with them. He reported that the Sarcee were "determined to remain where they were and die, sooner than return to the Blackfoot Crossing." He sent them south to Fort Macleod, where rations would be issued, but it wasn't until the police pulled down a few tipis that they actually left.

Bull Head, Sarcee chief, 1887. *Provincial Archives of Alberta P.109*

It was bitterly cold, and the trip—160 kilometres or so—took eleven days. Provisions were handed out as they arrived. Bull Head immediately began pressing for a reserve near Calgary. By the spring of 1881 everyone had grown weary of arguing with him. Once more the Sarcee were persuaded to return to their reserve on the Bow; they were assured that land would be ploughed and ready for planting when they arrived. Presumably the government intended to hire crews to do the work, but when the Sarcee arrived it had not been done. Once again Bull Head proved as good as his name. He petitioned Ottawa with his grievances, and the Sarcee were finally granted twenty-eight hundred hectares on the western outskirts of Calgary.

It was perhaps the shrewdest move any Native leader had ever made, but Bull Head would not live to see the results. The Sarcee submitted only half-heartedly to forced farming and ranching. There was little profit in it, and no excitement. Between 1891 and 1901 consumption claimed 65 members of the community. In 1896 alone there were twelve births and thirty deaths on the reserve. Contemporary photographs show Sarcee children in schoolrooms with their faces bandaged to cover tubercular sores. Bull Head died in 1911, perhaps in mourning, for his people continued to diminish. By 1924 the population was a mere 160, and there was no reason to believe it would increase.

As with most aboriginal peoples, however, their lot improved in proportion to the degree to which they were allowed to rule their own lives. With better health care and the relative autonomy of an elected chief and counsellors, the modern Sarcee have been able to exploit their proximity to one of the most vigorous cities in Canada while not losing sight of their history. They are involved in industry, cattle, real estate, and recreational facilities, and are pursuing a conscious effort to revive their traditional

Sarcee Indians in Calgary, 1889. *Glenbow-Alberta Institute NA-1004-1*

culture and lifestyle. The Sarcee Peoples Museum is a monument to their struggle and their success. Indian Days, held every summer, attracts visitors from across the continent, and for many years the Sarcee have been an essential part of the Calgary Stampede. Many are also active in the Anglican and Roman Catholic churches, but, like the early peoples of Europe, they have adapted the faith to their culture rather than vice versa, and incorporated Native values and celebrations into the life of the church.

From a low of 160 in 1924, the population has grown to over 800 today. Diamond Jenness expected them to be extinct within a hundred years. For a time it seemed that he would be proved right, but the progress of the Sarcee over the past half-century reminds us once again that the easy assumptions of Eurocentric scholars should be viewed with suspicion.

The Gros Ventre

THE NAME by which the Gros Ventre are commonly known is the result of a mistake. "Big belly" was an erroneous interpretation of their sign, which was communicated by the speaker moving a hand in front of his stomach. They were also known as *Atsina*, a Blackfoot term meaning "gut people." Both the sign and the word have been taken to mean that, no matter how much they were given, they always wanted more. But this, too, is mistaken, for the name had more to do with their abundant tattoos than with the size of their stomachs. In their own Algonquian language they are known as *Haaninin*, "chalk men"—a name to provoke the imagination, if nothing else.

The Gros Ventre were the fifth part of the Blackfoot confederacy, after the Siksikah, the Blood, the Peigan, and the Sarcee. They originally belonged to the Arapaho Nation that occupied the high plains between the Platte and Arkansas Rivers in the United States, an immense area that today crosses a half-dozen state boundaries between Arkansas and Wyoming. The Gros Ventre, too, spread themselves across a huge area of the northwestern plains. In the mid-eighteenth century their hunting grounds included much of southern Saskatchewan. In 1772 the explorer Matthew Cocking found them occupying the territory between the branches of the Saskatchewan River east of the Peigan, where they suffered the brunt of Assiniboine and Cree attacks against the confederacy.

Gros Ventre tipis near Fort Belknap, Montana, 1896. *Glenbow-Alberta Institute NA-1419-7*

Socially and politically, the Gros Ventre were organized along the same lines as the nations of the Blackfoot, with several age-graded warrior societies for men as well as an association for women. They celebrated the Sun Dance and other festivals with elaborate ritual. They lived in skin lodges and followed the buffalo herds. And, like the Blackfoot, they were less interested in the fur trade than in raiding their neighbours.

Severely weakened by the epidemics of the late eighteenth century, they were pushed south by the Assiniboine and the Cree. Then in 1793 the Cree wiped out a band of sixteen lodges of the Gros Ventre, who received little if any aid from the Blackfoot. Obviously, their alliance had not been secure. Knowing the Cree to be friendly with the fur traders, the Gros Ventre retaliated by harassing the trading posts along the Saskatchewan. In 1794 they looted and destroyed the Hudson's Bay Company post at South Branch House. This did not endear them to the traders, and life on the northwestern plains soon became too dangerous and uncomfortable to be endured. They fled south to join their Arapaho kinsmen, thus removing the buffer between the Blackfoot and the Cree, and for the first time placing the two powerful alliances in direct conflict.

In 1861 a quarrel over stolen horses severed finally and forever their ties with the Blackfoot confederacy, and the Gros Ventre ceased to have any further noticeable influence on the development of the Canadian plains. They now occupy a reservation in eastern Montana.

Gros Ventre woman preparing feast for grass dance festival, 1896. *Glenbow-Alberta Institute NA-1419-12*

The Nations of the Cree

....

F ROM LABRADOR to the Great Lakes, from the Great Lakes to Hudson Bay, and latterly from Hudson Bay to the Rocky Mountains, from the plains to the subarctic, the land that was to become Canada was dominated by the powerful and populous nation of the Cree. For the better part of two centuries they and their allies virtually controlled European trade and access to European technology across an area large enough to dwarf England and France together. It was from the Cree that the nations of the Blackfoot received their first firearms. It was through the Cree that pots, pans, cooking utensils, steel knives, and hatchets came to the peoples of the northwest a hundred years before any of them met a European.

The tribal name of the Cree evolved through various incarnations from a term that may have had little relevance for them in the first place. One version is that an Ojibwa word for a group of Indians who lived near James Bay was recorded by the French as *Kristineaux*. This was later abbreviated to Cree and applied to the whole nation. The anthropologist Diamond Jenness stated simply that *Kristineaux* was the "French form of a name, of unknown meaning, that a portion of the tribe applied to itself." Joseph F. Dion, too, in *My Tribe the Crees*, admitted to being "unaware of its meaning." Whatever its origins, many of the people who are officially known as Cree today only refer to themselves as such when they are communicating in English. Their own term is *Nehiyawak*, "exact people."

Scholars have divided the nation variously into Plains, Woodland, Swampy, and Moose Cree. Most writers do not differentiate between the subarctic branches, and refer to them all as Woodland Cree. Jenness stated simply that they can be divided into the Plains Cree and the "Woodland Cree, usually called Swampy Cree or Muskegon." Dion, while noting that "various white historians . . . have been carried away with themselves and mixed fiction with the truth," more or less agreed with Jenness:

> For ages past there has always been a marked distinction between the prairie people and those who resided in the wooded lands, hence the terms Plains Indians and Bush Crees. The latter clan often crossed over to the south and joined the summer hunts after the buffalo, but their meat diet was supplemented by fish in their home grounds. These two groups always got along very well . . .

They were all woodland people originally, speaking the Algonquian language of eastern Canada. The Cree claim that theirs is the parent tongue, not a dialect. It is a highly developed, complex language. According to Dion, there is a term for every branch of kinship and a word for every type of snow, and different forms of speech for men and women. The only words they have had to borrow from other languages, Dion claims, are "swear words."

Woodland Cree camp near present-day Edmonton, ca. 1898. *Provincial Archives of Alberta B.766*

In 1654 Huron and Ottawa Indians from New France made contact with the Cree and introduced them to European products. In 1730 La Vérendrye encountered in Manitoba "Cree of the mountains, prairies, and rivers," for they had by then begun moving onto the plains in response to the commercial imperatives of the fur trade. The search for furs and food, observed Andrew Graham, a Hudson's Bay Company trader, had caused the Cree "gradually to retire farther inland, until they came amongst the buffalo"—a classic British understatement, although Graham was a Scot. "Retire" was hardly an appropriate word to describe what the Cree were doing, and it was anything but gradual. As J.R. Miller has pointed out, the First Nations of Canada were "active agents of commercial, diplomatic, and military relations with the European newcomers and their Euro-Canadian descendants."

It is difficult to imagine how a civilization that had been flourishing for thousands of years could be abruptly transformed by the sartorial tastes of people across a distant ocean, but this seems to be what happened. The traders demanded more and more furs to clothe the wealthy and the fashionable of western Europe, and the Cree took it upon themselves to provide them—either directly through hunting and trapping, or as intermediaries, making huge profits as they bartered for robes and pelts among First Nations who were less providentially situated. Allied with the Assiniboine and armed with European weapons, they easily displaced any weaker groups that stood in their way. The acquisition of firearms by their enemies slowed them down, but their advance across the continent was really halted only by smallpox.

"None of us had the least idea of the desolation this dreadful disease had done," wrote David Thompson of an appalling scene he came upon in 1781. "We looked into the tents, in many of which they were all dead, and the stench was horrid . . . From what we could learn three-fifths had died of the disease."

Epidemics in the 1780s, the 1830s, and the 1860s reduced the Assiniboine by half, left thirty-one Mandan alive of a population of sixteen hundred, wiped out 90 percent of the Chipewyan, and two-thirds of the Blackfoot. Five hundred Gros Ventre died in a single month in 1837. The Cree were not immune. Joseph Dion wrote of a Cree war party invading a Siksikah camp at the beginning of the epidemic of 1869-70:

The Blackfoot [Siksikah] were suffering from smallpox which rendered them incapable of protecting themselves. The Crees were delighted and so plundered everything. Alas they barely made home when they too began to take sick and die. Their whole village was quickly infected, many died of broken backs, others were horribly disfigured with scabs, hence the name we gave that dreaded malady, *omikiwin*, the disease of scabs. It left a permanent brand on those it did not kill.

Although vaccination saved the Plains Cree from annihilation, smallpox overall killed more than half of them. Measles, diphtheria, and tuberculosis afflicted them no less, on the plains and in the forest, and in some places rivalled the mortality rates of smallpox.

In 1821 the rivalry between the Hudson's Bay Company and the North West Company came to an end, but it had exacted a dreadful price. In many places there weren't enough animals left to sustain a traditional lifestyle. The Woodland Cree, no strangers to famine, tried to subsist on what was left. On the plains their kin were no longer needed as interme-

The buffalo were hunted to near-extinction by the 1880s. This pile of buffalo bones near Gull Lake, SK, was gathered from the prairie for shipment by rail–probably to Minneapolis, where they would be ground up and made into fertilizer. *City of Vancouver Archives IN.P.79.N.123*

diaries, for there were trading posts throughout the west. They turned to selling meat and pemmican to the Europeans, a trade the Blackfoot had already established. In addition, the market for buffalo robes was expanding, and their hides were used for machinery belts in eastern factories. This, along with the advent of the European and American sports hunter, put increasing pressure on the buffalo and undoubtedly hastened the decline of the herds. By the end of the fur trade era the Cree had actually increased in number, but their economic and social options had been radically reduced. The buffalo were gone. The forests and parklands had been overhunted and overtrapped. Encouraged by the imperatives of commerce, they had chosen specialized roles for themselves—hunters, trappers, and intermediaries—but by doing so, they had unwittingly become dependent on the Hudson's Bay Company. When those roles were no longer viable, they became dependent on the government.

The Plains Cree

WHEN THEY LEFT THE FOREST to expand their empire onto the plains, many bands of Cree remained edge-of-the-woods people, venturing onto the prairie only to hunt buffalo. Many more, however, "retired farther inland," in Andrew Graham's delicate phrase, and embraced the horse culture of the eighteenth century as if they had been born to it.

Allied with the Blackfoot, they drove the Shoshoni and the Crow from the Canadian plains. When that alliance broke down, they renewed their ancient confederacy with the Assiniboine and launched raids against the Blackfoot. They spread across Alberta to the Peace River and south to the Missouri, and raided west through Blackfoot territory to the Rocky Mountains.

In the spring of 1869, while on a peace mission to the Blackfoot, the Cree diplomat Maskepetoon was murdered along with his entourage. The act was interpreted, rightly, as deliberate treachery, and while the attention of the nation was fixed on Louis Riel and his provisional government at Red River, a state of total war existed along the Cree-Blackfoot border from Fort Edmonton to the Missouri. As many as seven hundred violent deaths occurred on the northwest plains in this period, culminating in the battle of Oldman River where a force of six hundred to eight hundred Cree and Assiniboine soldiers led by Big Bear, Little Mountain, Little Pine, and Piapot were routed by a force of Blood and Peigan. Among the latter was one Jerry Potts, later to become famous as a guide and interpreter for the North-West Mounted Police. "You could fire with your eyes shut," he reported, "and would be sure to kill a Cree." In fact they killed over two hundred, while the Blood and Peigan lost less than forty.

It was the last plains war. Those the violence and the smallpox and the whisky hadn't killed, they had exhausted. The Cree sent tobacco to the Blackfoot in 1871, a ritual gesture of friendship. Thanks largely to the diplomacy of Crowfoot, head chief of the Siksikah, a peace was concluded that autumn. Henceforth the bands would follow the herds across the prairie without regard for territory or boundaries. It was, perhaps, as it should always have been. For the Cree, like all nations of the plains, were first and primarily buffalo hunters.

The number of bison, or buffalo, on the Great Plains before the Europeans arrived has been estimated, conservatively, at 60 million. They ranged from the Peace River in northern Alberta to Texas in the south, from the Appalachians in the east to the Rockies in the west. Until the last quarter of the nineteenth century they remained uncountable in their natural realm. As late as 1873 a party riding south from the Cypress Hills reported that it took them seven days to pass through a single grazing herd. Another group, camped by the Qu'Appelle River, took shelter in the brush when they heard the buffalo coming, then watched for twenty-four hours as the herd forded the river at a rate of several hundred a minute. An American boundary commissioner, climbing several hundred feet above the plain to get a wider view of a particular herd, reported that he could not see the limits of it in any direction.

At the time these enormous herds were observed by Europeans and their first- or second-generation descendants on the North American continent, the original peoples had been hunting the buffalo for a hundred centuries. They consumed its meat in enormous quantities. Its hide provided shelter and clothing. Its bones and sinews were put to hundreds of uses in the Native economy. The hunt was therefore of primary, even mystical, importance to the nations of the plains. Every aspect of it was controlled by ritual and ceremony, and there were severe penalties for any infraction of the rules. For man and woman alike, it was a test of skill and endurance. Even children were occasionally pressed into service, depending on the organization of the hunt.

After the great migration every year, the buffalo broke up into smaller herds for mating and grazing. A skilled hunter could put his ear to a gopher hole and hear a moving herd thirty kilometres away. If it was July, the rutting season, the bulls would be fighting each other or going after the cows, and the sound of their running was a deep hum in the distance. A running herd was difficult to intercept, but a grazing herd could be approached fairly easily. Buffalo haven't a keen sense of hearing, and they see better to the side than straight ahead. If the hunters remained downwind they could elude the animals' only acute sense and be reasonably sure of getting within rifle range or bow shot.

It was the horses that posed one of the chief difficulties in approaching a herd, for a trained buffalo horse was highly strung and easily spooked. Like stallions bred for racing, they were impossible to hold once the excitement started. With a herd within sight and smell, a high-spirited horse could easily startle the animals into flight before the hunters were ready.

The cows grazed at the front of the herd, so it was usually the bulls that first became aware of the hunters. Each animal stood as tall as a man at the shoulder, and weighed ten times more. They drew together in a horned phalanx, snorting and pawing the ground. As the hunters advanced, they began to run, pushing the cows ahead of them. But the meat of the bulls was stringy and tough. It was the cows that were prized, and the hunters had to break through the racing bulls to get to them.

The horse knew its job and expected the hunter to know his. If a rider was unseated during the run through the bulls, his chances of survival were virtually nonexistent. A buffalo would not intentionally trample a man if it saw him in time, nor would it gore him if he was lying flat on the ground. But a thousand running buffalo are not likely to step aside for a single human, and a hunter who fell off his horse onto the head of a bull could expect to be tossed in the air until there was not enough left of his body to catch on the animals' horns.

The hazards did not lessen once a hunter had made it through the bulls. Primitive firearms could blow his hands off if they weren't handled carefully, and it is difficult to do anything carefully in a crowd of stampeding buffalo. For that reason, being hit by a random bullet was also a danger. Arrows were safer, and actually more deadly. The Sarcee used bows of wild cherry and arrows of willow. The Cree used willow for the bow as well, preferably from a tree that had been killed by fire but was still standing. From two or three metres away, the hunter would aim at a point behind and below the left shoulder, that being the most direct path to the animal's heart. An arrow truly shot might penetrate her running body and come out the other side.

Mustatem Moutiapec, Cree Indian. The acquisition of the horse and firearms radically altered the nature of the hunt, trade, and warfare on the plains.
Glenbow-Alberta Institute NA–4595–9

The explorer and map-maker Peter Fidler observed a hunt in 1792:

Men killed several Cows by running them upon Horseback & shooting them with arrows. They are so expert at this business that they will ride along side of the Cow they mean to kill & while at full gallop will shoot an arrow into her heart & kill her upon the spot. Sometimes when they happen to miss their proper aim (which is very seldom) they will ride close up to the Buffalo . . . at full gallop & draw the arrow out & again shoot with it.

In this manner a skilled hunter could kill eight to ten buffalo in a day. According to plains historian Joseph Howard, however, even when the shooting was over, the danger wasn't:

> After the run—a mile or two—the hunter returned along his row, identifying animals he had shot by characteristic features of the carcass or of the wounds . . . The return ride was as dangerous as the original run because of the buffalo practice of playing possum; and recumbent buffalo, unlike domestic cattle, could spring up on all four feet at once. Animals only slightly wounded would lie as if dead until hunter and horse were almost upon them, then leap up and charge.

Other methods of killing buffalo were the *piskun* and the pound. The *piskun* was a cliff, the pound was a log corral, and the buffalo were driven over it or into it depending on the circumstances. Both methods were wasteful. In the former, a herd would be stampeded over a cliff where, if they didn't die outright, the animals would be crippled and easily killed. This took a large toll of calves, for which there was little use, and bulls, whose flesh was disagreeable. It also damaged the hides, bones, and tendons, and made each animal that much less useful.

To drive a herd into a pound demanded a certain skill, for the animals had to be steered in the right direction and at an appropriate speed. Men, women, and children would be positioned in two long lines spreading out from the gate of the pound. As the herd approached, they each stood up in turn, driving the animals closer and faster until they were running headlong down the neck of the human funnel into the enclosure at its end. But if the animals were started too fast, or if they were too frightened, they could easily swerve and trample the people who had been placed to guide them into the pound. Once enclosed, however, they were easily speared or shot.

These methods were largely abandoned when the plains nations acquired horses and firearms. The Cree, however, continued to rely on pounds until well into the nineteenth century. Like everything else concerning the hunt, the construction of the pound was regulated by tradition and ritual. Elaborate ceremonies accompanied the dedication of each new pound, and a medicine pole hung with offerings was raised in the centre. Song and prayer drew the buffalo near, and "Poundmaker" remained an honoured name among the Cree until the end of the nineteenth century. By then there were fewer than a thousand buffalo left on the North American continent.

The *Rupertsland and North-Western Territory Order* of 1870 was an Order-in-Council of the federal government whereby the Hudson's Bay Company sold its territories to the new Dominion of Canada. Also called the Deed of Surrender, it provided that, "Any claims of Indians to compensation for lands required for purposes of settlement shall be disposed of by the Canadian government in consultation with the Imperial Government; and the Company shall be relieved of all responsibility in respect to them."

In accordance with the Order, Treaty #2 was concluded with the Cree and the Saulteaux in the summer of 1871. The territory ceded was primarily in Manitoba, and the treaty provided, among other things, for 160 acres (65 hectares) of land for every five persons, annuity payments of three dollars per person, and protection from the sale of alcohol.

The meaning of "protection from the sale of alcohol" is unclear. Presumably the Cree and the Saulteaux wanted whisky traders kept out of their territory, and prosecuted if they were found selling alcohol to Natives, for they had suffered as much at the hands of these unscrupulous men as had any other nation of the plains.

Treaty #4, also signed by the Cree and the Saulteaux, followed in 1874, and included much of southern Saskatchewan. Annuity payments were raised to five dollars per person, and hunting and trapping rights were included. The Cree chief Piapot refused to sign, maintaining that the provisions of the treaty were not enough, and that the buffalo hunt should be restricted to Indians.

Elsewhere on the plains, it was increasingly apparent to Native leaders that the herds were failing and the fur trade was coming to an end. Subsistence farming on reserves seemed preferable to a slow death by starvation, which was surely the only alternative. Several Cree bands therefore petitioned the dominion for a treaty before incoming settlers could appropriate their lands. They wanted provisions for medical and famine relief, 640 acres (260 hectares) of land per family of five, protection from the sale of alcohol, agricultural aid, schools, hunting and fishing supplies, protection of their subsistence rights, and an annuity of five dollars per person. Most important, they wanted, like Piapot, to preserve the buffalo from further slaughter by non-Natives. Many of these provisions, including the last, were promised orally. Others were written into the subsequent treaty—#6, known as the Fort Carlton and Fort Pitt Treaty for the two places it was signed in 1876.

Poundmaker had spoken against entering treaty at Fort Carlton in

As immigration to the West increased, so did the government's desire to settle Native people on reserves. *Glenbow-Alberta Institute NA–249–42*

August 1876, but he did sign eventually. Though not yet a chief, his influence had been growing among the Cree since Crowfoot, head chief of the Siksikah, had adopted him as his foster son in 1873. Two years after his band had capitulated to the treaty, he was recognized as chief. A year later, in 1879, he took a reserve.

Big Bear was reluctant to sign Treaty #6, fearing the loss of Native autonomy and the acceptance of Canadian sovereignty. Treaty conditions seemed to him a guarantee of perpetual poverty and the destruction of the Cree way of life. At the very least, the compensation was insufficient to warrant his giving up the things he cherished. Big Bear was supported by Piapot and Little Pine, who had also refused to adhere to Treaty #6. The three leaders moved their bands into the Cypress Hills in search of game, and there began to press for contiguous reserves. The Department of Indian Affairs refused their requests, and in 1882 began to use the threat of withdrawing rations to drive them out of the Cypress Hills. Faced with starvation, they moved north where, one by one, they eventually accepted reserves. Big Bear took treaty in 1882, and two years later accepted a reserve in the Battleford district. "But his retreat," as J.R. Miller pointed out, "was merely a strategic withdrawal, not a surrender."

The aim of Cree leaders was to unite the First Nations of the plains

Negotiations for Treaty #6 at Fort Carlton, 1876. *Glenbow-Alberta Institute NA-1406-177*

and force the government to renegotiate the treaty, for many of its provisions had been violated or left unfulfilled, and many Natives felt they had been misled by the federal commissioners during negotiations. Not only were legitimate grievances ignored, but authorities were deliberately violating treaty provisions in order to force bands to submit to the policies of the Department of Indian Affairs. In 1884 Big Bear sent runners to the chiefs of the plains, calling on them to attend a great Sun Dance and Council at Little Pine Reserve near Battleford. This gathering, and others like it, was designed to unite through common ritual the different groups across the plains, including such hereditary enemies as the Blackfoot and the Cree. Twelve bands went on to a council at Duck Lake, attended by Louis Riel, and they drafted a petition detailing their grievances.

The government's attitude toward petitions, as both the Métis and the whites had cause to know, was one of almost aggressive apathy. Ottawa politicians had, to them, more important things on their minds than the distant west. On the eve of the 1885 rebellion, virtually every community on the plains was only a step away from radical action. An editorial in the February edition of the *Edmonton Bulletin*, reprinted in the *Prince Albert Times*, angrily denounced Ottawa and stated flatly that rebellion was the only way to make the politicians and the bureaucrats listen.

Leaders such as Big Bear and Piapot well understood the futility of taking up arms against the Canadian government. Their best chance of achieving their objectives, they knew, was in maintaining a united front.

Inevitably, there were those who couldn't wait. On 2 April 1885, militant members of Big Bear's band murdered nine whites at Frog Lake, and any support the Cree might have expected from disgruntled white settlers instantly vanished. Indeed, the government attempted, with a good deal of success, to characterize the incident as a general Native uprising in response to the successful action of the Métis at Duck Lake on 26 March. Big Bear managed to restore his authority, but by then it was too late. A general panic had set in among white settlers. Around Battleford, many of them fled to the fort for refuge, thus precipitating another unfortunate incident. Members of Poundmaker's band, on their way to the post in search of food, looted a number of abandoned homesteads near the fort. In subsequent histories, these events became known as the "Frog Lake Massacre" and the "Siege of Battleford."

Poundmaker retreated to his reserve, where he managed to defeat a punitive force led by Colonel W.D. Otter at Cut Knife Hill. He prevented his warriors from pursuing the retreating soldiers, but this act of good will was not deemed relevant at his trial. Big Bear spent a couple of months in the bush north of Frog Lake evading another punitive force led by General T.B. Strange. The soldiers never did find him. Poundmaker surrendered to General Middleton at Battleford on 26 May. Big Bear surrendered to the police at Fort Carlton on 2 July. He and Poundmaker were both convicted of treason felony and sentenced to three years' imprisonment. Joseph Dion wrote:

> I have gazed with pity and chagrin on moving pictures of grandfather Big Bear represented as a young active man leading his followers into battle. Why Big Bear was ready to die of old age at the time of the 1885 rebellion; he had tried desperately to dissuade his men from committing any deeds of aggression, and failed. His only fault was that he was chief and the trouble had to be pinned on someone.

Big Bear was released from prison in March 1887, sick, defeated, and utterly broken in spirit. He died the following January. Poundmaker served only one year of his sentence, but he too was broken in health and spirit when he went to visit his foster father, Crowfoot, shortly after his release. He died at Blackfoot Crossing in July 1886. In 1967 his remains were brought home by his fellow Cree of the Sweetgrass Reserve, and buried on Cut Knife Hill.

In the aftermath of the rebellion the Indian agent replaced the chief as

A group of North-West Rebellion participants, including (*back row, left to right*) Constable Black, Louis Cochin, Inspector R.B. Deane, Alexis André, and Beverly Robertson; (*front row*) Horse Child, Big Bear, Alexander Stewart, and Poundmaker. Big Bear and Poundmaker fought against unjust and unfulfilled treaty terms. *National Archives of Canada C1872*

the dominant personality on the reserve. Directed by the policies of Hayter Reed, who was named Commissioner of Indian Affairs in 1888, the explicit and contradictory goal of Indian agents across the plains was the assimilation of all Native peoples into the dominant white culture—as long as they didn't leave the reserve. Communal farming and the pooling of resources by Indian bands smacked of tribalism, and was officially discouraged. Successful Indian farmers, on the other hand, were encouraged, and sometimes forced, to "enfranchise" themselves—i.e., take private ownership of their property and surrender their status as Indians in exchange for obtaining the status of citizens.

There were not many successful Indian farmers during this period. By the turn of the century many Cree were just subsisting through a combination of hunting, fishing, farming, labouring for their white neighbours, and lining up for rations. Conditions gradually improved as one generation replaced another, both in Ottawa and on the reserves. But then the younger people who had been taken from their parents to be educated by the dominant culture were placed in conflict with the elders, who were struggling to retain a semblance of what they most cherished.

Modern conditions among the Cree are both alarming and hopeful. The abject poverty of some reserves is balanced by the prosperity of others. The surrender of some to alcohol and drug addiction, prostitution and crime, sexual abuse and suicide is balanced by the less-well-known successes of many others—successes often achieved against appalling odds, for politicians and bureaucrats even now are reluctant to grant Native Canadians the simple dignity of directing their own lives. Through it all the Cree have somehow managed to retain their Indian-ness—sure evidence that they will endure, and even prosper.

The Woodland Cree

THE CREE were among the first Natives to meet British fur traders in the 1600s. They appreciated immediately the advantages of metal knives and hatchets, utensils, and especially guns, and soon began to trap in earnest to supply the demands of the traders and procure the products of European technology. These nomadic families and bands bore little resemblance to the naïve and greedy children presented in much colonial literature. On the contrary, they were extremely selective in what they accepted for trade. They made it clear, for example, that they wanted firearms that would work

A Cree man, Johnny Bear, with peace pipe, Edmonton, *ca.* 1905–10. *Provincial Archives of Alberta B.907*

in the brutal subarctic winter, and they were no less particular in their choice of other goods. Beads, blankets, cloth, needles, and animal traps all had to meet their exacting standards before they would accept them for trade. Like their kin of the plains, they also assumed the role of intermediaries, enriching themselves at the expense of weaker or more distant communities. Some of them, the "Home Guard," lived around the posts in an area known as the plantation, and were chiefly engaged in supplying fresh meat to the traders.

Beyond the forts of the Hudson's Bay Company, the Cree expanded west and north as they became adept in the use of firearms. By the middle of the eighteenth century they dominated both Manitoba and Saskatchewan north of the Churchill River, and virtually all of northern Alberta. For generations they were the mainstay of the fur trade.

They had no strong tribal identity, no complex social structures, and no warrior or religious societies. The basic social unit was the family or the band. They hunted alone or in small groups, as the animals they sought were solitary creatures, or moved in small groups themselves. In the southern areas of their territory the Cree lived in lodges of birch bark, either dome-shaped like those of the Ojibwa or conical like those of the plains nations. Further north, where birch was both scarce and scrawny, they used pine bark or caribou hide.

Warfare was not as common among them as it was among their relatives on the plains, but they were as competent as any when occasion demanded. Alexander Mackenzie noted in 1801 that the Cree "had driven away the Natives of the Saskatchiwine and Missinipy rivers" and continued to push west "even till the Beaver Indians had procured guns, which was in the year 1782."

Alcohol probably killed more of them than firearms did. The Hudson's Bay Company at first used liquor sparingly, but even that had a demoralizing effect. The women seemed more vulnerable to it than the men. The men, in fact, viewed drunkenness as a contemptible state, for it made women jealous and violent, and caused them to neglect their children. But they eventually modified their opinions. "They are so addicted to drunkenness," wrote Andrew Graham in the 1770s, "that they practise every art to procure brandy, and had they free access to it, death only would put an end to their debauch, of which we have had instances." Graham was exaggerating from a sense of personal revulsion, but there can be little doubt that alcohol became, in the words of James Isham, another Bay trader, "the chief cause of their Ludness and bad way's they are now given to." The "bad way's" Isham referred to included prostitution and pimping, and their inevitable bedfellow, syphilis. Few European observers mentioned the fact that pimping and prostitution cannot flourish without customers; indeed, the Natives were far from alone in their "Ludness and bad way's."

When the North West Company came into competition with the Bay in the last quarter of the eighteenth century, it imported alcohol in quantity, deliberately exploiting the weakness of a race that had no resistance to it in order to gain a competitive edge. The Hudson's Bay Company responded in kind, and the Natives succumbed in proportion to the ruthlessness of the competition between the two companies. It wasn't until the merger of the competitors in 1821 that the Hudson's Bay Company once again tried to limit and even prohibit the use of alcohol, but by then a major wound had been inflicted on the woodland culture.

Even so, the Cree were among the most skilful hunters on the continent. "An Indian came to hunt for us," the explorer David Thompson noted in his journal, "and on looking about thought the ground good for moose, and told us to make no noise." The hunter set off into the forest. When he came back, he reported that "he had seen the place a doe moose had been feeding in the beginning of May." This was early October. Over the next two days he followed the evidence of her progress through three more months, to the beginning of September. Then one day he announced that he had been as close to her as he could get without giving himself away. He needed "a gale of wind," he said, to mask his movements and his scent before he could get close enough to kill her, and "when this took place he set off early, and shot the moose deer."

The Woodland Cree had little choice but to be skilful hunters and gatherers; the alternative was famine. They took deer, elk, moose, woodland caribou, beaver, and bear as they were available, and in winter they turned to hare. They did not disdain fish, as did many buffalo hunters. They speared them, or cast lines with hooks, but the bulk of the fish they ate was caught by women using nets. They also gathered birds' eggs, and added the sap of birch and poplar to their diet in season. In *Our Grandmothers' Lives*, Glecia Bear recalls that her mother would set snares for rabbits, "or she would go out and shoot partridges in the bush." They ate the soft parts of water plants, and gathered roots when they were available. Antoine Jibeau, a survivor of the last smallpox epidemic, spoke of having a meal of "whitefish and potatoes" the night his family became infected. If he was eating potatoes, then obviously they were involved in agriculture of some kind as well. And the ubiquitous saskatoon berries were used in pemmican and other preparations throughout Cree territory.

Because of the harsh climate, they did not wear tanned hides but caribou fur, or woven hare skin. They adorned themselves with tattoos, an uncommon practice among Algonquian people, and the women had a widespread reputation for beauty, "their Eyes Large and Grey yet Lively and Sparkling very Bewitchen," according to James Isham, whose enthusiasm led him to take "a plurality of wives" in addition to the one he had left in Britain.

Like other Algonquian peoples, the Cree treated widows and orphans with great kindness. Old people who could no longer keep up with the

A group of Cree at Regina, SK, *ca.* 1909. *Glenbow-Alberta Institute NA-1255-48*

band, however, would generally be abandoned, or sometimes killed at their own request. This was a common practice among nomadic people, whose survival depended on their ability to keep moving. Any hindrance to a band's mobility might place the whole community in jeopardy, so the aged and the infirm would expect to sacrifice themselves for the good of the group.

Every decade or so, natural fluctuations in the animal population raised the spectre of starvation. Early traders mention instances of cannibalism among the Indians often enough that they must be given credence, and the legends of the Cree are replete with tales of supernatural creatures who feast on human flesh.

Windigo was an evil spirit who took many forms. Norval Morrisseau's painting of the creature depicts a brown giant edged in black, consuming peculiar hybrid beings with beaver tails and human shapes painted on their backs. Anyone who dreamt of Windigo, he wrote, was in great danger, for he might "from time to time turn into Windigo so that the demon might satisfy his great hunger for human flesh." In other tales, Windigo can enter a human body and transform its rightful occupant into a cannibal, who would then have to be disposed of by his or her relatives.

Other creatures, though terrifying, served a purpose that was more cautionary than evil or psychotic. The spectral skeleton Pakakos, for example, attacked hunters who killed more than they needed, or who wounded animals and let them escape.

Treaty #8, taking in much of northern Saskatchewan and all of

Wetigo (Mask) Dance, Sweetgrass Reserve, Saskatchewan, 1939. *Saskatchewan Archives Board R–A.7671*

northern Alberta, was negotiated in 1898. The first of the northern treaties, it was signed by the Woodland Cree, the Beaver, and the Chipewyan, who asked for more liberal terms than had been included in southern treaties: assistance for people in need, aid in difficult times, education without religious interference, and exemption from taxes and military service. Indian Commissioner David Laird assured the signators that these things were government policy, and there was no need to include them in the treaty. By all accounts, Laird was a trusted and honourable man, but government policies change, and subsequent difficulties in interpreting the intent of this and other treaties have led many to wish that the terms had been written down. Only recently have governments begun to recognize the validity of oral promises made to the signators at the time of signing. Treaty #8 did include trapping rights, as many Natives were still living a traditional lifestyle.

Treaty #9 was signed by the Cree and the Ojibwa and affected, along with a great deal of northern Ontario, a minimal wedge of northeastern Manitoba. From 1899 to 1927 the First Nations of the area had been petitioning the government for aid in maintaining their land and livelihood. The treaty was signed in 1905; the adhesion of 1929-30 extended its area of authority to its present boundaries. Its provisions included an annuity of four dollars per person, the allocation of reserves, and the protection of hunting, fishing, and trapping rights.

Treaty #10 covered much of central and northeastern Saskatchewan, and a wedge of eastcentral Alberta. Its signators included the Cree and the Chipewyan. It was 1906, the year after the province of Saskatchewan had been created, and the government wanted to establish clear land title for purposes of development. An annuity of five dollars per person was provided for, as well as assistance in agriculture, a rather unrealistic option in the subarctic.

The fur trade continued in the north for decades after it had run its course on the plains and in the parkland. To some extent it continues today, although it has long since ceased to provide a stable or an adequate income. The nations of western Europe, which conceived and gave birth to the fur trade, have disowned it in its dotage. Still, with their long history of collaboration with Europeans and Canadians, the Woodland Cree are better prepared than many to confront the demands of technological society—and sometimes, perhaps, repudiate them—as they work toward self-government and economic development.

This is not to say that their success depends on collaboration with Euro-Canadian society. On the contrary, since the arrival of the first explorers, the success of Europeans in the north has depended on collaboration with the Natives.

The Saulteaux

THE SAULTEAUX are a composite of Ojibwa peoples who came together at Sault Sainte-Marie in the seventeenth century to trap and trade. Their name is from the French *Saulteurs*, "people of the rapids," although they have been known by other names. "Saulteaux, who refer to themselves as Bungi," according to one anthropologist, "could as well be called the Plains Ojibwa." In fact, they often are.

They speak a central Algonquian language closely related to the Cree, with whom they were allied. Like the Cree, they were lured west by the fur trade and eventually took up life on the plains. Like the Cree, too, many remained on the edges of the parkland, venturing onto the prairie only to hunt buffalo. The trader and map-maker Peter Fidler, with heroic disregard for the conventions of spelling and grammar, wrote of them in his journal:

> These Indians are not originally natives of these Parts, but were first introduced by the North West Company about the year 1797—before this there were a very few Stragglers—they being then Industerous they was induced by the Reports of the Canadians that Beaver abounded here & was invited to leave their original Lands about the Rain Lake & the Western borders of Lake Superior—now they finding this Country so much more plentiful in Provisions than their own & the Beaver being plentiful—they have become quite habituated to these parts & I believe will never return to their own Lands again.

Fidler, a Hudson's Bay Company employee, may have been ascribing more intention to the North West Company than was the case. The Saulteaux would have moved west anyway, with their allies, the Cree. After the merger of the companies in 1821, many of the Woodland Cree, having lost their status as intermediaries, moved onto the plains to follow the buffalo. The Saulteaux moved in behind them. They were a thorough people, and made good use of lands the Cree had thought trapped out. Thus the Plains Ojibwa to some extent became the Woodland Ojibwa, but such classifications often don't mean much. During the nomadic period tribal territories could expand or contract by the size of a small European country within a generation. Boundaries were as changeable as the weather, and frequently overlapped.

Whether they occupied the plains or the parkland, or both, the Saulteaux never completely abandoned their woodland heritage. They preserved their religion and folklore, and adapted from the plains cultures those beliefs and festivals, such as the Sun Dance, that seemed necessary for survival. But fish remained a significant part of their diet, which was unusual for a plains people, and they retained their belief in the supernatural powers of their shamans. People from other communities frequently sought their medicines and love potions, to the annoyance of Christians who were trying to convert them. A certain naïve arrogance is apparent in the missionary Robert Rundle's assessment:

> Several of the Souteaux Indians left in the morning to hunt buffalo because I had preached on the previous evening against their idolatries. They pretended to have intercourse with familiar spirits & thereby held the other Indians in terror with their pretended divination & enchantments.

To the Natives, of course, their divinations and enchantments were no more "pretended" than were the missionaries' prayers. But more enduring than love potions and sorcery was their contribution to art, for it was the Saulteaux and the Cree who introduced the floral designs of the woodland to the traditional, geometric art of the plains. This was most apparent on tipi covers and shields, which traditionally depicted images from the hunt or a vision, but its most subtle and beautiful manifestation was in clothing and personal adornment. With painstaking quill embroidery, and later beadwork as new materials became available, moccasins and gowns and items of functional or purely decorative purpose burst into exquisite bloom at the hands of Saulteaux women. The distinctive vision and style of many modern Native artists—painters, sculptors, and printmakers—can be traced back to the inspiration and the dexterous hands of their grandmothers.

Men and women alike wore charms and ornaments, the men with

Saulteaux woman and child, ca. 1885. *Provincial Archives of Manitoba N12794*

somewhat more panache. They had a particular passion for silver. According to Peter Fidler, the young men were "very flashy & decorated with a variety of silver ornaments," including "necklaces made of Whampum about 2 Inches broad, arm and wrist bands with gorgets," as well as "Scarlet Leggins garnished with Ribbands and a number of small Brooches, which is very tastefully arranged."

In the mid-nineteenth century, large camps of Saulteaux, Cree,

Assiniboine, and Métis gathered for the buffalo hunt or the Sun Dance, and there was a fluid movement of customs and practices. The Saulteaux, in common with the others, painted their faces and worked grease into their hair. The men spent more time on their appearance than the women, often grooming themselves for hours. Some wore two braids, others four, but women generally had a single braid or let their hair hang loose, perhaps with a strip of vermilion painted along the part. Hair brushes were made from porcupine tails; a wooden handle was thrust inside the freshly severed appendage so that the skin would "shrink-wrap" it as it dried.

The Saulteaux and the Cree harvested wild rice, as their descendants do to this day. David Thompson described the harvest beginning in early September. A "thin birch rind" was laid over the bottom of a canoe, and "a man lightly clothed, or naked, places himself in the middle," then, "with a hand on each side, seizes the stocks and knocks the ears of rice against the inside of the canoe." He could collect ten or twelve bushels before having to unload the canoe, which could be filled three times in a day. While women unloaded the harvest, the man "smokes his pipe, sings a song; and returns to collect another canoe load."

Following Confederation in 1867, the treaty process began with the newly independent Dominion of Canada, though not at the dominion's behest. As was the case more often than not, it was the Natives who pointed up the need for land settlements, often with the advice and counsel of missionaries and Hudson's Bay Company employees. Treaty #1 was the result of persistent lobbying by the Saulteaux. They were aware that the Hudson's Bay Company had sold its land—Saulteaux land—to Canada. They disputed the terms of the Selkirk Treaty whereby land had been purchased for the Red River settlement, and they had presented their concerns to William McDougall when he tried to enter Red River as its governor in 1869. McDougall was willing to consider a treaty in exchange for an alliance against the Métis, whom he was finding rather troublesome, but he was recalled before he could set the process in motion. The Saulteaux knew that their lifestyle and territory were in jeopardy, and they threatened to interfere with western settlement if their grievances were not dealt with.

Negotiations began in the summer of 1871. The Indians wanted a reserve roughly two-thirds the size of the present province of Manitoba; at 160 acres (65 hectares) per family of five, the treaty provided somewhat less. The Indians asked for annuities of three dollars per person, as well as schools, agricultural aid, and protection from the sale of alcohol. As with subsequent treaties, some of these requests were written down, others were promised orally. The treaty was signed later that year. By 1875 the Saulteaux had still not received what they had been promised, and they petitioned the government to fulfil its obligations. Ottawa eventually revised the treaty, increasing their equipment and livestock, and boosting their annuity to five dollars per year.

Treaty #2, taking in a portion of southcentral Manitoba and a wedge of southeastern Saskatchewan, was also signed in 1871. It contained much the same provisions as Treaty #1, with the addition of oral promises for the retention of hunting, fishing, and trapping rights. The signators were the Saulteaux and the Cree.

Treaty #3 took in a large portion of southwestern Ontario and a much smaller piece of southeastern Manitoba. The Saulteaux in that area had held out for more favourable terms through successive attempts in 1871 and 1872. They knew that settlers would have to pass through their territory on their way west, and pointed out that there might be some unpleasantness if Native concerns were not addressed first. Consequently, the Saulteaux received farm animals and equipment, schools, annuities, protection from the sale of alcohol, and a written guarantee of their hunting and fishing rights.

Treaty #4, again signed by the Saulteaux and the Cree, was concluded at Fort Qu'Appelle in 1874. The territory affected took in a portion of southwestern Manitoba, most of southern Saskatchewan, and part of southeastern Alberta. Its terms and provisions were similar to those of Treaty #3, except that trapping rights were added to hunting rights, as the Saulteaux were active in the fur trade.

Treaty #5 was concluded with the Cree and the Saulteaux in 1875. Signed in the Lake Winnipeg area, it covered mostly central Manitoba, but in 1908 was revised to include the north of the province. Again, it was much like Treaty #3. At first it restricted reserve acreage, but later brought it into line with the other treaties.

Most treaties contained later additions called "adhesions." If provincial boundaries extended north, for example, the Natives in those areas could be included in an adhesion. If certain bands did not sign the treaty, for whatever reason, they could sign later, accepting the same rights and responsibilities. The option remains open to individuals and bands today.

Unlike the nations of the Blackfoot, who were highly organized both politically and socially, the Saulteaux and the Cree lacked a coherent tribal structure. This cannot be judged either good or bad, for a people develop

Saulteaux family, upper Assiniboine Reserve, 1889. *Provincial Archives of Manitoba N12793*

the kind of governance that will be appropriate to their situation and numbers. The consequences for the Cree and the Saulteaux were that they signed five treaties and are now scattered in small reserves across the three prairie provinces. Their economies are as various as the skills and determination of individual bands and their ability to exploit their resources. The larger nation of the Ojibwa, however, is emerging in modern times with the beginnings of a shared identity, and many now prefer to be called *Anishinabe*, meaning "person" or "first man." The Anishinabe nation, then, is a term that has the potentiality to unite the scattered speakers of the central Algonquian languages of the Ojibwa.

The Dakota

············

A CCORDING TO LEGEND the Dakota, like Adam, emerged from the soil of the earth. A single man awoke one morning on the Great Plains, facing the sun. All about him, the land was soft with primeval mud. There were no mountains, no trees, no rivers. Eventually the sun hardened the mud and strengthened the man, and he sprang from the earth with grace and freedom—gifts of the Spirit that had created him. From this man came the Dakota nation, who lived and died on this same plain for thousands of years before the Europeans came.

Scholars tell a somewhat less interesting story of migrations, internal conflicts, thwarted uprisings and, rarely, heroic victories. What is certain is that the Dakota who live in Canada today arrived as refugees from the United States in the last century, and are known in the larger society as the Sioux. That term, however, is the French version of an Ojibwa word meaning "adders" or "snakes"—metaphorically, enemies. Their own designation, Dakota, means "allies," and is now commonly used to distinguish them from the wider Siouan language family. Strictly speaking, though, only the eastern groups are Dakota. Among the central groups, from whom sprang the Assiniboine, the dialect supplants the "D" with an "N"—hence, Nakota. In the plains dialect, the "N" becomes an "L" and the nation is the Lakota.

Archæological evidence indicates that the Dakota were resident in western Manitoba and eastern Saskatchewan before AD 900, but in the intervening millennium they became a distinctly American people. Nonetheless, it was to Canada they came when they sought peace and fair

(Facing page): Dakota family at their hunting camp in Saskatchewan, 1885.
Glenbow-Alberta Institute NA-2294-20

treatment. They referred to the forty-ninth parallel as the "medicine line," for it distinguished a land of refuge from one in which they were hunted like animals.

They had not always come in peace. In the eighteenth and nineteenth centuries, war parties frequently ranged north into Canada. Alexander Henry recorded attacks by the Dakota on the Cree at Red River in 1800 and on the Saulteaux at Portage la Prairie in 1806. For their part, the Dakota opposed all attempts by the Saulteaux, the Assiniboine, and the Blackfoot to expand their territory south. They were a populous and highly organized nation, ranging from the woodlands of Minnesota to the plains of South Dakota.

It was the Minnesota Uprising that brought the first Dakota to Canada. By a treaty in 1851 they had ceded the greater part of their territory west of the Mississippi. In 1858 their reservation was cut in half, reinforcing a general mood among the Dakota that they had been deceived by the American government. They had long resented official attempts to turn them into farmers. In the summer of 1862 a delay in the payment of annuities was the spark that led to a general uprising. Three hundred and fifty white settlers were killed. Little Crow, the principal leader, was eventually defeated at Wood Lake, and the Dakota, fearing reprisals, fled west and north. Those who came to Manitoba joined the Métis in the buffalo hunt, trying to avoid a renewal of hostilities with their traditional enemies, the Saulteaux. Eventually they followed the declining buffalo into Saskatchewan.

In 1873 the federal cabinet, recognizing that the Dakota intended to stay, passed two Orders-in-Council. One acknowledged the Dakota to be under the protection of the British flag, and therefore recognized them as status Indians. The other laid out a land policy: 80 acres (32 hectares) per family would be granted the Dakota bands resident in Canada, and the reserves were to be well north of the new international boundary. The government was in no hurry to put its policy into action, however, and it was some time before all the Dakota had received their reserves and the material assistance promised them on settlement. By far the majority of Dakota resident in Canada today are the descendants of these refugees from the Minnesota Uprising.

A treaty in 1868 had granted to the Lakota "forever" the land around the sacred Black Hills of South Dakota. Six years later gold was discovered, and the government repudiated the treaty. The Lakota and the Cheyenne prepared for war. In June 1876, Sitting Bull annihilated the United States

7th Cavalry under General George Armstrong Custer. Although it was a brilliant victory, the Lakota chief realized that he could not prevail against the armies of the United States, and many of his people fled north into Canada. By the end of 1876, several thousand Lakota were camped in southwestern Saskatchewan. The following spring Sitting Bull himself arrived, and assured the North-West Mounted Police that his people wanted only sanctuary and an opportunity to settle. Since the Lakota had no claim on Canadian lands, however, they were given neither reserves nor rations. In 1881 Sitting Bull retired to North Dakota, where he was killed in 1890. The few families who stayed behind, determined to hang onto their new life in Canada, were eventually assigned reserves.

The Dakota and Lakota in Canada have been expected for the most part to make their own future. They never signed a treaty, and have thus not had many of the privileges and rights accorded other plains nations. Numbering about twenty-five hundred in Canada today, they have become farmers, ranchers, wood-workers, and labourers, and have enjoyed success at small-scale resource management.

The Iroquois

....

THE IROQUOIS of the eastern woodlands had begun to use steel traps in the late eighteenth century, and the North West Company judged they could increase the harvest of furs dramatically if they convinced some Iroquois to come and work for them. The company was right. The Iroquois were keen and efficient workers, and thought to be more "civilized" than the local Natives. Women played prominent social and political roles in the matrilineal society of the Iroquois. Aside from being "responsible for agricultural operations," as J.R. Miller has pointed out, "chieftainship was hereditary among families of certain female lines, and the prominent women of the tribe had much to say about selecting the individual male who would become chief on the death of a leader."

In 1800 David Thompson reported that the Iroquois "now spread themselves over these countries, and as they destroyed the Beaver, moved forwards to the northward and westward. For several years all these Indians were rich . . . " They were also unwelcome. A second group was brought in on three-year contracts in 1801, "to complete the destruction of the beaver," but shortly after they arrived fourteen of them were set upon by a party of Gros Ventre and killed. In 1818 a band of Carrier Indians from the British Columbia interior killed an Iroquois whom they judged to be infringing on their territory. In 1827 *Tête Jaune*, or Yellowhead, an Iroquois trapper and diplomat for whom the mountain pass was named, was murdered along with his brother by local Indians.

Despite the hazardous working conditions, many of the Iroquois men who came west under contract to the fur trading companies chose to remain when their obligations had been fulfilled, although no women had accompanied them. The men worked as free agents in the foothills and in the north, and eventually numbered in the hundreds. As they came west,

John Callihoo *(left)*, chief of Michel's Reserve, founded the Indian Association of Alberta. *Glenbow-Alberta Institute NA-3137-1*

they brought their tribal practices, and spoke the Iroquoian dialect of the eastern woodlands. They painted themselves for battle and held a war dance before a raid. They had their own pipe dance and gambling games. But they tended to marry Cree women, and by mid-century a Catholic missionary observed that the Iroquoian language was virtually extinct among them. They spoke Cree or French, and had more or less settled in the Jasper and Grand Cache area of Alberta.

They didn't show up at Fort Carlton or Fort Pitt when Treaty #6 was signed, but they did endorse an adhesion two years later. In 1880 they took up residence on Michel's Reserve near Edmonton, where they were admired for their agricultural skills. One federal inspector remarked that the crops were so excellent and the fields so well kept that "one cannot realize that he is driving through an Indian reserve." One can almost fancy, he declared, no doubt believing that he was paying them a compliment, that "he is passing through some of the newly settled districts of Ontario."

At the turn of the century the agent for Michel's Reserve reported that, "as no women came with the original immigrants, it is obvious that the Iroquois blood in this generation is attenuated to the vanishing point." They had lost their language, he continued, "and if they retain any tribal characteristics they have become so feeble that the ordinary observer of Indian manners is unable to discern them."

Such crude generalizations did not endear the agent to the Indians, and the band's leaders were constantly scrapping with their federally appointed guardians. Government policy was aimed at the assimilation of the aboriginal population across Canada, but the authorities were peculiarly reluctant to allow the Iroquois of Michel's Reserve to do just that. The Iroquois, for their part, were sufficiently self-assured to organize a political action group, the Indian Association of Alberta, in 1939. John Callihoo, an Iroquois chief and a leading proponent of the movement, was nicknamed "the lawyer"—it was not meant as a compliment—by officials of the Indian Department with whom he was in frequent conflict.

So fed up did the Iroquois become with bureaucratic interference that three times they attempted to remove their reserve from government control. In 1931, again in 1949, and finally—and successfully—in 1958 they renounced their legal status. Their land became private property. Michel's Reserve ceased to be a reserve, and those who lived on it ceased legally to be Indians.

The Kootenay

K OOTENAIAN is a language isolate; it is common to no other nation. At one time it was thought there were only 30 or 40 speakers of it left on the planet. More recent estimates put the figure closer to 160. The upper and lower branches of the Kootenay are divided more or less equally between Canada and the United States. The Upper Kootenay are properly a British Columbia people, but throughout the first half of the eighteenth century at least one band of Kootenay, and possibly others, occupied southwestern Alberta, where they hunted buffalo and acquired the characteristics of a plains culture. Archæological evidence suggests that the Kootenay occupied southern Alberta as long as two thousand years ago, and this is verified by their own oral traditions.

In social and political organization, the Kootenay resembled the nations of the plains more than those of British Columbia. They had no clans, no caste system, and no secret societies. A warrior society policed the camp and the hunt. Other societies, one of them restricted to women, were dedicated to religious purposes.

The Kootenay reckoned descent through the female line, but their leadership was patriarchal nonetheless. A special chief was elected in times of war or for the hunt, but his position terminated when it was no longer necessary. Women and children taken in war were enslaved, but they were treated well and eventually absorbed into the community.

Kootenaian mythology, not unlike the Peigan, regarded the earth as a great island beneath the dome of the sky. The Kootenay paid honour to the sun, and offered it prayers and tobacco smoke before setting off to war. A warrior might chop off the tip of his finger to appease the sun, or tear his flesh in an act of self-mortification, not unlike the flagellants of mediæval Christendom. Like Christians, too, they believed in the

Kootenay woman on horse with travois, nd. *Glenbow-Alberta Institute NA-714-156*

immortality of the soul, and held an explicit belief in the resurrection of the dead. They were convinced that the dead would rise at Lake Pend d'Oreille, and staged religious festivals there at auspicious times.

Following the practice of plains nations, young people underwent a period of seclusion at adolescence, seeking supernatural visions through prayer and supplication. The practice extended to girls as well as boys, though it is difficult for the Euro-Canadian to reconcile this apparent gender equality with reports that the Kootenay practised polygamy. The European abhorrence of multiple and simultaneous spouses, however, took little account of First Nations' attitudes toward sexuality, which was quite different from the European ideal, and the social situations of many Natives, for whom both polygamy and polyandry might be sensible solutions to practical problems.

Kootenay family in British Columbia, ca. 1900. *Glenbow-Alberta Institute NA-1141-2*

Kootenay tradition speaks of a smallpox epidemic that wiped out their people east of the Rockies. Blackfoot tradition speaks of a war party that drove the Kootenay back over the mountains. Whatever the cause, they left, but returned to the plains year by year to take part in the buffalo hunt.

Because of their isolation, the Kootenay experienced little of the stresses of white settlement until the latter half of the nineteenth century, by which time many had already taken to ranching and raising horses. Before European contact their population was estimated at twelve hundred, roughly half of them living in Canada. They have diminished but little since then, although their language is close to extinction.

The Crow

························

T HE ACQUISITION OF HORSES caused many First Nations to abandon agricultural communities for the less sedentary lifestyle of the mounted nomad. The North American continent was the scene of massive population shifts as the horse made its way north from band to band and nation to nation during the seventeenth and eighteenth centuries. The Crow emerged in this period as nomadic hunters and warriors, mostly in Montana and Wyoming, but steadily pushing northward into Alberta and Saskatchewan.

Blackfoot tradition asserts that the Crow commanded the territory south of the Bow River until they were driven out in the 1700s. There is some question as to how long they had been there—a few decades or several generations—but there is no tradition among the Crow of any significant period spent north of the "medicine line," the forty-ninth parallel. Now resident in Montana, where the Siksikah chief Crowfoot made his famous raid and took his name, the Crow continued to make war against the Blackfoot even after they had settled onto reserves in the 1880s.

A Crow Indian scout, ca. 1880. *Glenbow-Alberta Institute NA–207–47*

The Shoshoni

....

T HE SIGN for the Shoshoni nation was a snake, and they were
known as the Snake Indians among the Blackfoot. They spoke an
Uto-Aztecan language, and historically occupied the mountain areas of
Idaho and Wyoming. Seasonal residents of the grasslands and the plateau,
they were among the first to acquire the horse, and made good use of it in
the hunt and in war. Their aim was not so much expansionist as it was
acquisitive; they were active in the slave trade and liked to take captives,
who had a high trading value among the Spanish to the south, and even
the French. When the Blackfoot acquired guns they were finally able to
drive the Shoshoni out of their territory.

Even so, the sinew-backed Shoshoni bow was more accurate and more
reliable than firearms until the mid-nineteenth century. Alexander Henry
the Younger reported in 1811 that a Peigan would trade a gun or even a
horse for such a bow. By then the Shoshoni had retreated south, but they
remained a preferred enemy of the nations of the Blackfoot for several
generations afterward.

(Facing page): A Shoshoni woman *(left)* and a Cree woman at Fort Union,
North Dakota, as sketched by Karl Bodner, 1883. *Glenbow-Alberta Institute*
NA–2347–3

The Chipewyan

CHIPEWYAN is a Cree term for "pointed skins" and refers to the way they cut and wore their shirts, with tails front and back. Because of the difficulties of the Athapaskan language, early interpreters sometimes failed to communicate the fact that the tails belonged to the shirts, not the people, and for some years it was held among the credulous that a race of half-human creatures inhabited the boreal forest and the barren lands.

The Chipewyan were a populous and widespread nation of the subarctic. At their height they occupied territory from the Churchill River north to the tundra, and from Hudson Bay on the east as far west as Great Slave Lake, including the woodlands of northern Manitoba, Saskatchewan, and part of Alberta. Yet they had little notion of community or government. Language was the only real link between the small bands that travelled and intermarried and the larger nation. Their concept of leadership was casual, changeable, and entirely appropriate to their numbers and circumstances: a complex system of government is not a reliable measure of a people's development. In a culture that valued flexibility and personal autonomy, a wise woman or an experienced hunter were respected, but they had no real authority. Their suggestions were taken or ignored according to the situation.

The Chipewyan had no organized warfare, either, although they had no hesitation in falling upon their enemies when the occasion demanded it. In such measure as enemies were defined, the Cree to the south were simply *ena*, "enemy," while the Inuit to the north were *hotél ena*, "enemies of the flat area." When the Hudson's Bay Company established a post at Churchill in 1717 and supplied them with firearms, the Chipewyan proceeded to drive the coastal Inuit north. They also denied the Dogrib and

Red Bird and his wife, a Chipewyan couple, *ca.* 1900. *Provincial Archives of Manitoba N133342*

the Yellowknife access to the post, forcing these northwestern nations to trade their furs for a fraction of their value to the Chipewyan. With the Woodland Cree to the south they established an uneasy peace, although they continued to skirmish with one section of that nation on and off until 1760.

With the establishment of inland posts by the fur companies, the Chipewyan role of intermediary for the less fortunately situated Dogrib and Yellowknife nations largely ceased. From 1788, when Fort Chipewyan was established on Lake Athabasca, there was peace among the Athapaskan speakers, collectively known as the Dene, and the Cree. By that time, the Chipewyan had been devastated by smallpox—it carried off fully 90 percent of them—and had little heart for further conflict.

Caribou in the north was treated much as buffalo in the south; it was eaten fresh or dried, roasted or boiled, or pounded into pemmican. Sometimes it was eaten raw, after the fashion of the Inuit. It provided food, clothing, and shelter, and served a multitude of other uses. A complete suit of winter clothing might take eight or ten hides, and a similar number was necessary to supply a family with a lodge covering, lines and nets for fishing, snowshoe lacing, and nooses for snares. The hides were at their best in August and September, and many animals were killed for their hides at that time, with only the choicest parts eaten.

The Chipewyan pursued the caribou season by season, impounding them in the woods when the snow was deep and following them onto the barren grounds in spring. They speared or shot them as they floundered across open water in the summer and when they took shelter in the forest in winter. Pounds, which were constructed along migration routes, contained a mass of fences and gates, with a snare in every opening. Samuel Hearne reportedly saw woodland pounds "that were not less than a mile round," and brush fences of "not less than two or three miles" through which the animals were funnelled into the pound. One can only imagine the effort and ingenuity necessary to build a structure nearly two kilometres wide and three to five kilometres long.

They hunted buffalo, moose, musk oxen, and smaller game when caribou were not available, and supplemented their diet with berries, edible bulbs, and the tender shoots of young plants in season. They snared waterfowl and arctic hare. "When the land is short of Deer," wrote David Thompson, "they take to the Lakes to angle Trout or Pike at which they are very expert." They also used nets of *babiche*, a kind of rawhide webbing, or they painstakingly wove a net from the inner bark of the willow, which could be shredded and twisted into strings.

The Chipewyan were highly mobile, and had to be careful not to own too much. "The real wants of these people," wrote Hearne, "are few and easily supplied; a hatchet, an ice-chisel, a file, and a knife, are all that is required to enable them, with a little industry, to procure a comfortable livelihood." Dwellings were temporary and portable, consisting of a framework of poles covered with caribou skins, or sometimes bark. They slept on bearskins and caribou robes, ate from bark dishes, and used baskets of birch bark or woven roots. A woman's personal possessions would include awls and needles, spoons, ladles, and skin scrapers. A man's would consist of those implements of bone, horn, or antler mentioned by Hearne, though a wealthy man might have copper tools purchased from the Yellowknife people to the northwest.

In summer they travelled on foot or by spruce bark canoe. In winter they used snowshoes (the Chipewyan were the only people who made right- and left-foot snowshoes), and the women pulled the family goods on toboggans. They also carried the children, either in moss-lined bags or Inuit fashion on their backs. Dogs were employed as pack animals.

The business of staying alive through the long, cold winters and the brief, warm summers precluded much time for amusement. A small feast was held when someone died, a somewhat larger feast on an eclipse of the moon. Otherwise, they observed those ceremonies common to the Cree or dictated by their shamans. Despite Hearne's allusions to "a comfortable livelihood," there was little physical comfort in their lives.

Female children were separated from their male companions at the age of eight or nine to create their own community. At the onset of puberty, they lived in seclusion while older women instructed them in the ways and wisdom of maturity. The ritual included a strict diet of dried meat, and they could drink only through a hollow bone. They used a "scratching stick" to avoid touching their bodies. During their menstrual periods, women were forbidden to walk on a hunting trail or on ice where men were fishing, or to step over the personal belongings of a hunter. This taboo was not from fear of uncleanness, as many early chroniclers assumed. Rather, the Chipewyan held in awe the life-creating power of women, signified by the menstrual period that comes once in each lunar cycle. The taboo was rooted in power, not pollution.

Even so, women did most of the heavy work, and they were the first to suffer in seasons of famine. They were "made for labour," according to Matonabbee, Samuel Hearne's Chipewyan guide; "one of them can carry, or haul, as much as two men can do." Matonabbee had seven wives himself, "maintained at a trifling expense," and declared that "the very licking of their fingers in scarce times is sufficient for their subsistence."

In the eighteenth century, Samuel Hearne, David Thompson, and Alexander Mackenzie all commented on the suffering and drudgery in the women's lives. Later accounts, however, failed to find such harsh treatment of women among the Chipewyan. Perhaps, after the devastation of smallpox, the survivors realized they would have to depend on one another, man and woman alike, if they were not to perish utterly. Perhaps, too, early observers misunderstood or exaggerated what they saw, so different was it from their own experience. Certainly, Matonabbee was guilty of hyperbole in the caricature he presented to Hearne.

Chipewyan religion appeared either simple or nonexistent to the Europeans who first attempted to study it. In fact, it was deceptively complex. They recognized no deities and offered no sacrifices or public prayers. But the whole of life was, in Judæo-Christian terms, an act of prayer. They did not differentiate between the sacred and the secular; all was sacred, although it is doubtful they would have used that term. Animism embraces the notion that plants, animals, and inanimate objects all have souls, and humankind occupies no privileged position amongst them. A person's relationship to the material and spiritual world is no different from that of a caribou or a tree. Spirits inhabit all of creation, and one's relationship to them is defined by rituals, taboos, and other observances.

It was the shaman's task to keep the forces of creation in balance, to

See-Seep-Ace (Little Duck) *(centre)*, Chipewyan Chief, Rousseau River, *ca.* 1900. *Provincial Archives of Manitoba N13344*

ward off evil and placate offended spirits. The shaman was initiated through dreams and mystical visions, the latter characteristically brought on by fasting and supplication. The shaman was often able to heal others, physically or spiritually, to bring good fortune and prosperity to the band, and to guide young and old alike on their individual vision quests. Alternatively, a shaman might be possessed of great malevolence, and the mythology of the subarctic is replete with colourful and cautionary tales. As a prudent measure, the shaman was treated with respect, and often enjoyed more personal influence than other members of the band. Although shamans directed the spiritual life of the band as occasion demanded, anyone could communicate with the supernatural through dreams and visions.

According to one observer, the Chipewyan believed that the souls of the dead travelled in a stone canoe to an island where game was plentiful and famine unknown. If the person had sinned greatly in this life, the canoe would sink before it got to the island, and the unfortunate human soul would flounder forever in the water. A few souls might be reborn after a time, but the Chipewyan were generally indifferent to the implications of reincarnation.

The bodies of the dead were dealt with in a variety of ways, depending on the circumstances and, to a certain extent, on the influences of neighbouring communities. The corpse was often cremated, along with a few earthly possessions. Alternatively, it might be raised on a scaffold in the custom of plains nations, or covered with stones in the Inuit manner. Sometimes the necessity of moving on was greater than the need to deal respectfully with the dead, and the community would then be compelled to abandon the deceased to be devoured by scavengers.

Missionaries in the mid-nineteenth century found the Chipewyan ready for conversion. Indeed, Anglicans and Roman Catholics alike enjoyed such success that a visitor to Fort Chipewyan in 1899 reported that "all the Indians we met were with rare exceptions professing Christians, and showed evidences of the work which missionaries have carried on among them for many years." More recent observers have remarked that the Chipewyan may simply have incorporated Christ into their belief system alongside the other spirits.

In 1898 the Chipewyan signed Treaty #8, along with the Cree and the Beaver. It covered a large area from northeastern British Columbia to Great Slave Lake and down to northcentral Saskatchewan. The signators asked for more liberal terms than had been included in southern treaties, and the Chipewyan negotiator, according to commissioner David Laird, displayed "considerable keenness of intellect and much practical sense in pressing the claims of his band." The treaty incorporated trapping rights as well as a provision that allowed the signators to obtain land in individual allotments, as many were living a traditional lifestyle and had no wish to confine themselves to a reserve. Treaty #10 took in the remainder of northern Saskatchewan, and contained much the same provisions. It was signed by the Cree and the Chipewyan in 1906.

In the 1920s the increasing use of aviation effectively ended the isolation of northern communities, and the resultant rise in commercial fishing, tourism, prospecting, and resource extraction offered opportunities and temptations alike. For the first time since the advent of the fur trade, the Chipewyan were in a position to materially alter their lifestyle.

In the 1960s, government policies designed to improve life for the Dene had the effect of forcing many of them to relocate to permanent settlements. Only there could they receive family allowance, old-age pensions, and the benefits of improved housing, education, and health care. Often, too, it was only there they could be near their children, who had been removed to residential schools. A century of experience should have alerted the various levels of government to the problems that inevitably follow upon such policies—culture shock, dislocation and alienation, disruption of social patterns, difficulties in switching from a subsistence to a cash economy, and the resultant horrors of alcoholism, drug abuse, and family violence. But it didn't.

The fur trade continues to some extent, and some Chipewyan have returned to it—as a part-time venture, at least—reestablishing their ties to the caribou and the land. Others have sought new opportunities both on and off the reserve. From near-extinction, they have recovered to a population of some eighty-four hundred.

The Beaver

A CCORDING TO ONE SOURCE, the Athapaskan term for the Peace River was *Tsades*, "river of beavers," from which the community derived its name, *Tsattine*, "dwellers among the beavers." Alternatively, Beaver was the name of a single band, the *Tsadunne*, which early explorers applied to the whole nation, but the Beaver as a whole were known as *Dunexa*, "our people." The latter has a greater ring of authenticity, if only because so many First Nations refer to themselves as "people" of one sort or another—"prairie people," "real people," "earth people," "many people"—and it is easy to imagine how, in the difficult Athapaskan tongue, a term might be transcribed by one interpreter as *Tsattine* and by another as *Tsadunne*.

According to Alexander Mackenzie, the Beaver once commanded an area roughly defined on the north by the Peace River, on the south by Lesser Slave Lake, on the east by the present Alberta-Saskatchewan border, and on the west by the present town of Peace River. Immediately to the south were the Sarcee, a branch of the Beaver whose territory extended to the North Saskatchewan. Some time prior to 1760, the Woodland Cree, newly armed with rifles from the traders on Hudson Bay, moved west into the Mackenzie basin. The Slavey and the Beaver retreated before them. The Cree drove a wedge between eastern and western bands of the Beaver and separated the Sarcee entirely from the parent community.

One problem with this account is that it contradicts Sarcee tradition, which indicates an internal cause for their separation from the Beaver. Be that as it may, the Beaver were eventually confined to the valley of the Peace River. The eastern portion made peace with the Cree, and by so doing gave the river its name: *Unijigah*, Peace River. Inland posts built by the competing fur companies met all their needs, and they

Beaver Indian band near the Peace River, ca. 1899. *Glenbow-Alberta Institute NA-1255-43*

made no subsequent attempts to occupy their former territory.

The eastern Beaver adopted the dress and customs of their neighbours, to a large extent, and soon appeared to European observers to be a reflection of the Cree in all things but language. The western branch ascended the Peace River, displacing the Sekani and maintaining their distinctive traditions and customs.

The Beaver did not depend on the beaver as much as their name would imply. Certainly, the animals were important for both meat and fur; a traveller in 1872 reported that "not less than 20,000 beavers are annually killed by the tribe on the waters of the Peace River." But the lifestyle of the people was based more on larger game. Although not a horse culture, some bands had obtained horses from the Cree and hunted buffalo as the plains nations did. More frequently they were unmounted and drove them into pounds. They hunted moose in the forest, and in the winter impounded caribou. They preferred snares for trapping, and they favoured moose over other meat. Fishing they considered beneath the dignity of a hunter, according to European observers, but the importance of a hunter's dignity seemed to vary with the availability of game. In any case, women were equally involved in the gathering and preparation of food, and a number of early photographs show them fishing quite contentedly. It is inconceivable that any group of people eking a living out of the subarctic would ignore such an abundant and nourishing source of food.

In common with other Athapaskan people, the Beaver had no strong tribal ties but travelled in independent bands, each with its own territory, coming together in larger groups for summer celebrations and ceremonies. They lived in the conical tents common throughout the Mackenzie basin, but often discarded them in the summer for temporary shelters of brush or simple lean-tos. Aside from those few bands who had horses, they travelled on foot or in canoes made of spruce bark in the summer, and on snowshoes in the winter.

The women were highly skilled in treating hides, but they gave up traditional clothing fairly early; in 1809 a trader reported that "the great part of them are now cloathed with European goods." They generally used flint for knives and arrowheads, though moose horn and beaver teeth were also used. They hunted with spears and bows until they acquired firearms in 1782. Before European contact, they fished with a hook of bone and a line of sinew or rawhide. They cooked by means of hot stones in vessels of spruce bark or tightly woven roots; it is hard to imagine the skill and patience such weaving must have demanded. Latterly they used birch bark, which was easier to shape and make waterproof. In much of this they were not markedly different from other peoples of the subarctic.

Alexander Mackenzie characterized the Beaver religion as being "of a very contracted nature," and claimed that he had "never witnessed any ceremony of devotion which they had not borrowed from the Kristeneaux, their feasts and fasts being in imitation of that people." An anthropologist in the early twentieth century described a semi-annual offering of food and prayer among the Beaver, but subsequent observers have echoed Mackenzie in ascribing it to the Cree. Even acknowledging the difficulties of judging the religious practices of another by one's own—difficulties that went largely unacknowledged by Europeans—Mackenzie and those who came after were grossly oversimplifying what was in fact a complex and pervasive belief system.

The Beaver religion was based on a belief in guardian spirits and a future life. Their creation myth is remarkably similar to the account found in the book of Genesis. Yaquesati, the androgynous "being that sits in the spirit realm," thought the world into existence, divided land from sea, and created the plants and the animals, including humankind, endowing First Person with some of the creative power of the spirit realm. First Person, like Adam, misused this power and brought forth monsters. But whereas Adam loosed the monster of sin into the world, First Person created literal monsters that proceeded to prey on humankind. Eventually it was necessary for Yaquesati to send Usakindji, a great spirit being, to subdue the monsters and carve their bodies up into the present form of the animals.

Girls and boys alike were prepared from an early age to be sent into the bush on vision quests. There they were to seek what one writer has called "the essence of the outer reality." It may come in the form of a spirit animal who will give them a song, instructions for a particular task, or guidance in other matters. These visions were not to be revealed to others; rather, they were to be regarded as individual revelations and reflected on privately. Some time following puberty, the man or woman would begin to assemble a medicine bundle, with images or charms related to the supernatural aid they received as children.

Communal hunts and war parties were led by "dreamers" who could find an enemy camp, predict the success of a hunt, cure the sick, and ward off evil. They also counselled and taught, and prepared the bands for the changes to be expected from contact with European society.

Marriage among the Beaver demanded a definite commitment. It was the custom for a young man to serve his in-laws and hunt for them for twelve to eighteen months after he had taken their daughter as his wife. Alternatively, he served them until his first child was born.

Funerals, too, were elaborate. The Beaver deposited their deceased on platforms or in trees. In terms reminiscent of an Irish wake, European observers described how friends and relations would then engage in displays of mourning and grief. Sometimes they discarded or destroyed their property. The women would cut their hair, and sometimes slice off the end of a finger to assuage their sorrow.

After the merger of the North West Company and the Hudson Bay Company in 1821, many inland posts were closed as a cost-cutting measure. The decision, driven solely by market considerations, was taken without regard for the Natives who had become dependent on them. In retaliation, the Beaver attacked one post on the Peace River that was scheduled for closure, killing five company officials. The company retaliated by closing all the posts in the area. The Beaver outwaited them. As one observer noted, "No men in this land of hunters hunt better than the Beavers." Quite simply, the company could not afford to keep them away.

The Beaver were signators to Treaty #8 in 1898, surrendering their lands in exchange for reserves, annuities, and hunting and trapping rights. Over the years they had not escaped the disease and starvation that afflicted others, and their population had been in decline since the eighteenth century. Before European contact, it was estimated at approximately 1,500. By 1790 Alexander Mackenzie estimated their numbers were closer to 1,000. A missionary priest counted 800 in 1889. In the 1960s they were down to 560 on three reserves in northwestern Alberta. Much of their traditional land

Beaver Indian tipi in winter, Peace River area, ca. 1910. *Provincial Archives of Manitoba (Glenbow-Alberta Institute neg. # NA-1315-23)*

has been given over to farming and resource extraction; hunting and trapping is no longer possible except in the extreme north.

The anthropologist Jenness portrayed the Dene of the Mackenzie Valley as less virile than others, lacking in stamina and self-confidence. "They had scattered like sheep before the advance of the Crees," he wrote. They had "evaded in terror the Eskimo who occasionally ascended the river." White civilization had not come to them suddenly, nor had it required revolutionary changes. But they "lacked the vigour to react to the stimulus and are slowly fading away in despair."

Against this ill-considered verdict must be placed two things: the statement of a nineteenth-century trader who characterized the Beaver as "a peaceable and quiet People and perhaps the most honest of any on the face of the earth," and the fact that, in the past quarter century, their population has almost doubled. As Antonia Mills wrote in *The First Ones*, "For many generations now, the White society has assumed that the answer to the Indian problem is really in assimilation of the Indian population into the White man's world." But assimilation is "a two-way street," she continued, and Euro-Canadians must eventually learn "that they themselves could profit from understanding and even assimilating elements" of the Beaver cosmology.

The Slavey

······················

T HE SLAVEY are an Athapaskan-speaking people of northern Alberta, British Columbia, and the Northwest Territories. The name by which they are known in English is a translation of the Cree *Awokanak*, meaning "slaves." Europeans, at first contact, took it to be a term of derision, or simply an indication of their timidity. Among themselves they are *Acha'ottine*, "woodland people."

In the early eighteenth century they were close neighbours of the Beaver, their territory running west from the Slave River to take in much of the Mackenzie Valley. When the Cree invaded, the Slavey retreated down the Mackenzie, and at the end of the century were chiefly found west of Great Slave Lake.

Like all peoples of the subarctic, they developed systems of governance appropriate to their numbers and situation. For the Slavey, this meant living in independent bands with no observable leadership over the whole nation. Each band elected an experienced warrior to lead them in times of conflict, but the office was terminated once it had served its purpose. A council of hunters decided local quarrels in consultation with elders of both sexes.

Overall, the Slavey were considered a peaceful and inoffensive people, fond of story-telling and dancing, and, to European eyes, much kinder amongst themselves than other nations of the subarctic: they were not seen to abandon the sick and the aged, and the men and women treated one another with indulgence and respect. The sexes shared many household tasks, as well as the hunting and gathering basic to their survival.

The Slavey were truly people of the forest. They hunted moose and woodland caribou, neither of which are herd animals, but had to be tracked and hunted one by one. There were no drives, no pounds, and no

Slavey woman fishing through the ice on Hay River, NWT. *Glenbow-Alberta Institute NA-4433-31*

mass killings. Rather, they ran down big game on snowshoes, trapping them in deep snow, or snared them in summer. They took any game, large or small, in snares. They caught beaver in wooden traps when the water was open, and broke into their lodges in winter. Fish made up half their diet, and was especially important in winter when moose and caribou were scarce. They ate it fresh or dried, roasted over an open fire, or boiled in vessels of woven spruce roots using the hot stone method. They also ate birds' eggs, lynx, muskrat, rabbit, squirrel, and waterfowl, as well as cranberries and raspberries. But they avoided the barren lands, even when caribou were plentiful there.

Like the Beaver, young Slavey men worked for their in-laws on getting married, hunting and fishing for twelve months or more to keep them fed and clothed. Slavey men were reportedly more considerate of their mates than were their contemporaries in the Beaver and Chipewyan communities. With the unavoidable exception of childbirth, Slavey men did the heaviest work themselves, preparing the lodge and gathering firewood, and helping carry the household goods when the band was on the move.

Their clothing was similar to that of the Chipewyan and the Beaver—a caribou skin shirt with the hair left on, leggings extending from a belt at the waist, and moccasins attached to the leggings—but it was distinguished by fringes and ornaments in moose hair and dyed porcupine quills. Where caribou and moose were less plentiful, they wore garments of woven hare skin. Both sexes wore armlets, belts, and bracelets of leather embroidered with quills in exquisite detail; the quillwork largely gave way to beads as European trade goods became available, but some women have preserved the art of dyeing and weaving porcupine quills as a traditional expression of Slavey values. Men also wore necklaces of polished caribou antler, and sometimes a goose quill or a wooden plug through the nose. On those relatively rare occasions when they went to war, they sported headdresses of feathers or bear claws, painted wooden shields, and a unique kind of body armour of woven willow twigs.

In summer they lived in conical houses covered with brush or spruce bark. Two families generally pitched their lodges facing each other, so they

Slavey women tanning hides at Hay River, NWT, ca. 1896–1908. *Glenbow-Alberta Institute NA-4433-29*

could share an entrance and a fire. In winter they constructed low cabins of poles chinked with moss and a roof of spruce boughs.

Before European contact they had stone adzes for cutting timber, beaver tooth knives, clubs of caribou antler, and spears, daggers, and arrows with points of bone or antler. A wealthier hunter might have copper arrowheads purchased from the neighbouring Yellowknife or Dogrib people.

Slavey animism was based on spirit guardians and the vision quest, and, according to European observers, they had a reputation as powerful sorcerers. For that reason their more bellicose neighbours seldom ventured to attack them. They also differed somewhat from other Dene peoples in their approach to death. If death was imminent, a sufferer would confess his or her wrongdoings to a shaman, perhaps in the hope of delaying the mortal hour, but more probably as a means of purging the impurities of soul that might hinder progress in the afterlife where, aided by loon and otter spirits, the soul passed through the earth and crossed a great lake to start life anew in another world. The bodies of the dead were placed on scaffolds or, more elaborately, covered with leaves or snow and left with their property, a funerary hut erected over them to discourage scavengers.

The Slavey of Alberta, British Columbia, and a portion of the Northwest Territories were signators to Treaty #8 in 1898, and various bands continued to sign adhesions to the treaty until 1911. It was not until 1921 that Treaty #11 was negotiated with the Slavey farther north. Their population at that time was slightly over thirteen hundred—a minimal gain over the estimate of their numbers before European contact. By World War II they had been reduced to eight hundred by tuberculosis, influenza, and other diseases.

World War II was itself a trial. The Alaska highway opened up remote territory for the first time to non-Natives, and by the end of the war some Dene had become a minority in their own lands. After the war the traditional way of life broke down as the fur trade collapsed and people began to move into towns to take advantage of government programs and educational opportunities. Some people moved away entirely, seeking an urban future in the cities of Alberta. Others remained to labour in the oil fields or take up commercial fishing. With adequate health care the Slavey population has increased to over four thousand, and recent evidence suggests that they are to some extent recovering a traditional lifestyle.

The Sekani

························

T HE SEKANI, "people of the rocks," are an Athapaskan-speaking
people who occupied the basins of the Finlay and Parsnip Rivers
and the valley of the Peace River as far east as the present town of that
name. They appear to have separated from the Beaver quite recently, for
in many externals they are virtually indistinguishable, although some
western bands had begun to take on coastal influences at the time of
European contact and were holding potlatches, the gift-giving ceremonies
practised by the coastal nations. In the late eighteenth century they were
driven west, either with the Beaver or ahead of them as they retreated from
the expansionist Cree.

Their first white contact was not until 1824, and then it was with the
unfortunate Samuel Black, one of the few Nor'Westers the reorganized
Hudson's Bay Company refused to employ in 1821. Eventually he was
taken on, but he was always unpopular with the Natives, and in 1841 was
murdered at Kamloops.

Sekani was the name of a single band on McLeod Lake. They had no
name for the entire nation, and the identification of some nomadic bands
of the area with the Sekani is quite arbitrary. Like the Slavey, they were a
forest people. They had no permanent villages, but followed the seasonal
movements of the caribou and other animals. They maintained trade
alliances with the Slavey and the Beaver to the east, and with the Carrier
and the Tahltan to the west. Their chief products were furs and tanned
hides, for which they were justly admired. Trading posts established in
Sekani territory shortly after contact were largely ignored as the Sekani
continued to obtain European trade goods from the coast through
Tsimshian and Carrier intermediaries.

Marriage was regulated by degrees of blood relationship. The Sekani permitted both polygamy and polyandry and, like the Beaver and the Slavey, the Sekani husband had to provide for his in-laws for ten to twelve months after marriage, or until his first child was born. Young Sekani couples, however, asserted their independence immediately upon marriage by building a separate lodge for themselves.

The Sekani held that the human and the animal world were linked in some mysterious manner, and that animals had special powers they might grant humankind if they were approached correctly. Children of the community received their spirit guardian through visions brought on by fasting and supplication. The guardian—an animal or a bird—could be called upon in times of great need. Adults might be granted other guardian spirits, whose aid they could rely on at all times. A man might then become a shaman. Girls underwent a period of seclusion in adolescence, and were subsequently treated with the awe and respect due their life-bearing powers, with its consequent taboos and periodic restrictions.

In the 1870s a gold strike triggered major cultural disruptions as the Natives were swamped with newcomers. The Sekani were not as affected as their Athapaskan kin to the west, but they were generally demoralized by disease in the nineteenth century. Their population at the time of European contact was estimated at more than a thousand. By the late 1980s it had fallen to less than seven hundred.

(Overleaf): Sekani man, 1934. Sekani husbands had to provide for their in-laws for ten to twelve months after marriage, or until their first child was born. *Glenbow-Alberta Institute NA-1040-55*

Works Cited

Note: All the quotations used in this book are taken from the works below, as primary or secondary sources.

Ahenakew, Freda, and H.C. Wolfart, eds. & trans. *Our Grandmothers' Lives As Told in Their Own Words*. Saskatoon: Fifth House Publishers, 1992.

Andrist, Ralph K. *The Long Death: The Last Days of the Plains Indians*. New York: Collier Books, 1964.

Bebbington, Julia M. *Quillwork of the Plains/Le "Travail aux Piquants" des Indiens des Plaines*. Calgary: Glenbow-Alberta Institute, 1982.

Brizinski, Peggy. *Knots in a String: An Introduction to Native Studies in Canada*. Second edition. Saskatoon: University Extension Press, University of Saskatchewan, 1993.

Colombo, John Robert, ed. *Windigo: An Anthology of Fact and Fantastic Fiction*. Saskatoon: Western Producer Prairie Books, 1982.

Commissioners of the Royal North-West Mounted Police. *Settlers and Rebels: Being the Official Reports to Parliament of the Activities of the Royal North-West Mounted Police Force from 1882–1885*. Facsimile edition. Toronto: Coles Publishing Company, 1973.

Dempsey, Hugh A. *Indian Tribes of Alberta*. Calgary: Glenbow-Alberta Institute, 1988.

Dickason, Olive Patricia. *Canada's First Nations*. Toronto: McClelland & Stewart Inc., 1992.

Dion, Joseph F. *My Tribe the Crees*. Calgary: Glenbow-Alberta Institute, 1979.

Francis, R. Douglas. *Images of the West*. Saskatoon: Western Producer Prairie Books, 1989.

—— and Howard Palmer, eds. *The Prairie West: Historical Readings*. Edmonton: Pica Pica Press, 1985.

Friesen, Gerald. *The Canadian Prairies: A History*. Toronto: University of Toronto Press, 1987.

Howard, Joseph. *Strange Empire: Louis Riel and the Métis People*. Toronto: James Lewis & Samuel, 1974.

Jenness, Diamond. *The Indians of Canada*. Toronto: University of Toronto Press, 1977.

Kennedy, Dan (Ochankugahe). *Recollections of an Assiniboine Chief*. Toronto: McClelland & Stewart Inc., 1972.

Kerr, D.G.G. *Historical Atlas of Canada*. Third revised edition. Don Mills: Thomas Nelson & Sons (Canada) Ltd., 1975.

Leechman, Douglas. *Native Tribes of Canada*. Toronto: W.J. Gage & Company Ltd., nd.

McCourt, Edward. *Saskatchewan*. Toronto: Macmillan of Canada, 1968.

McInnis, Edgar. *Canada: A Political and Social History*. Toronto: Holt, Rinehart & Winston of Canada Ltd., 1969.

McMillan, Alan D. *Native Peoples and Cultures of Canada: An Anthropological Overview*. Vancouver: Douglas & McIntyre, 1988.

Miller, David R., Carl Beal, James Dempsey, and R. Wesley Heber, eds. *The First Ones: Readings in Indian/Native Studies*. Piapot Reserve #75, Craven, Sask.: Saskatchewan Indian Federated College Press, 1992.

Miller, J.R., *Skyscrapers Hide the Heavens: A History of Indian–White Relations in Canada*. Toronto: University of Toronto Press, 1989.

Morrison, R. Bruce, and C. Roderick Wilson, eds. *Native Peoples: The Canadian Experience*. Toronto: McClelland & Stewart Inc., 1989.

Mountain Horse, Mike. *My People the Bloods*. Calgary: Glenbow-Alberta Institute and Blood Tribal Council, 1989.

Rees, Ronald. *New and Naked Land: Making the Prairies Home*. Saskatoon: Western Producer Prairie Books, 1988.

Stocken, H.W. Gibbon. *Among the Blackfoot and Sarcee*. Calgary: Glenbow-Alberta Institute, 1976.

Surtees, Robert J. *The Original People*. Toronto: Holt, Rinehart & Winston of Canada Ltd., 1971.

Van Kirk, Sylvia. *"Many Tender Ties": Women in Fur-Trade Society, 1670–1870*. Winnipeg: Watson & Dwyer Publishing Ltd., 1993.

Woodcock, George. *The Canadians*. Don Mills: Fitzhenry and Whiteside Ltd., 1979.

Further Reading

Bloomfield, Leonard. *Sacred Stories of the Sweet Grass Cree*. 1930. Reprint. Saskatoon: Fifth House Publishers, 1993.

Brown, Dee. *Bury My Heart at Wounded Knee: An Indian History of the American West*. New York: Holt, Rinehart & Winston, 1970.

Bruchac, Joseph, and Michael J. Caduto. *The Native Stories from Keepers of the Earth*. Canadian edition. Saskatoon: Fifth House Publishers, 1991.

Flanagan, Thomas. *Louis "David" Riel: "Prophet of the New World."* Toronto: University of Toronto Press, 1979.